"Some books inform, others inspire, but few ignite! From its opening pages *Stockdale Paradox Christianity* ignites a blazing fire that both incinerates the façade of complacent Christianity and sparks a holy hunger in the reader to crash hell's gates by the Holy Spirit's power. It lays out a clear, insightful, and Spirit-inspired path for transformation from orthodox profession about the Spirit to dynamic life in the Spirit. It is a prophetic call to cultural impact."

—EARL COLEY, Pastor, Grace Assembly, Los Angeles

"*Stockdale Paradox Christianity* is for every church that wants to break out of the current stagnant cultural compromise. Steve Johnson has stewarded well this revelation from the Lord to release true riches from heaven, the power of the Holy Spirit to witness, and the fullness of the glorious church that Jesus has in mind. Both a confirming and convicting read, which are keys to true revival and another great awakening. This book will stir you to desire again to partner with God for his kingdom to come and his will to be done. I recommend this book for every pastor, church leader, and Christ follower who wants to see heaven come to earth through the power of the Holy Spirit. Thank you, Steve, for tapping into this revelation from God."

—LOUIE TREVINO, Lead Pastor, Harbor Christian Center

"*Stockdale Paradox Christianity* is a bold and timely call for the church to rediscover its prophetic voice in an age of compromise. With clarity, conviction, and spiritual grit, it challenges believers to face the hard truths of our cultural moment without losing faith in God's ultimate victory. Drawing from the powerful example of Admiral James Stockdale, this book urges Christians to combine unshakable hope with honest self-examination—and to stand courageously for the truth when the world demands surrender. Every pastor, leader, and believer who longs to see the church regain her strength and integrity should read this."

—JOHN E. JOHNSON, Transition Pastor, Legacy Transition Group

Stockdale Paradox Christianity

Stockdale Paradox Christianity

From Ghosting to Gatecrashing

∽

STEVE W. JOHNSON

Foreword by J. P. MORELAND

WIPF & STOCK · Eugene, Oregon

STOCKDALE PARADOX CHRISTIANITY
From Ghosting to Gatecrashing

Copyright © 2025 Steve W. Johnson. All rights reserved. Except for brief quotations in critical publications or reviews, no part of this book may be reproduced in any manner without prior written permission from the publisher. Write: Permissions, Wipf and Stock Publishers, 199 W. 8th Ave., Suite 3, Eugene, OR 97401.

Wipf & Stock
An Imprint of Wipf and Stock Publishers
199 W. 8th Ave., Suite 3
Eugene, OR 97401

www.wipfandstock.com

PAPERBACK ISBN: 979-8-3852-6171-0
HARDCOVER ISBN: 979-8-3852-6172-7
EBOOK ISBN: 979-8-3852-6173-4

Scripture quotations are from the Holman Christian Standard Bible® (HCSB), Copyright © 1999, 2000, 2002, 2003, 2009 by Holman Bible Publishers.
Used by permission. Holman Christian Standard Bible®, Holman CSB®, and HCSB® are federally registered trademarks of Holman Bible Publishers.

This book is lovingly dedicated
to my mentor and friend, Dr. J. P. Moreland,
whose life and teaching have shaped my journey of faith beyond words

You must never confuse faith that you will prevail in the end . . .
with the discipline to confront the most brutal facts of your current reality.

—Vice Admiral James Stockdale

Contents

List of Illustrations x

Acknowledgments xi

Foreword xiii

Introduction xv

SECTION ONE: *Crisis of Capitulation*

1. Cultural Drift 5
2. Not the Way It's Supposed to Be 23
3. Ghosted: Silence of the Shepherds 38

SECTION TWO: *Kingdom Triangle Algorithm*

4. Spirit Apex 58
5. Christians Have Lost Their Minds! 74
6. Shalom Soul vs. the Empty Self 94
7. Power Protocol 107

SECTION THREE: *Crashing the Gates—Rescuing the Captives*

8. Sisu: Beyond Grit 126
9. Standing While Others Bow 139
10. Stockholm or Stockdale . . . the Choice Is Yours! 148

Bibliography 161

List of Illustrations

Figure 1: Kingdom Triangle Diagram 60

Acknowledgments

I FIRST GIVE THANKS to the Holy Spirit, whose presence compelled me to write these words and whose power sustains the vision behind this book. Without his guidance, this work would remain lifeless notes instead of a living call.

To my beloved wife, Leila, thank you for your patience, encouragement, and steadfast love. You have carried this journey with me in ways no one else could see, and your faith has been a constant anchor. Your Finnish Sisu always challenges me to do my best.

I am deeply grateful to Dr. J. P. Moreland, who first inspired me nearly two decades ago and whose mentorship shaped both my dissertation and my life. Your passion for truth sharpened my own. You kept me tethered to the reality that this book is not about ideas alone, but about taking back ground for the kingdom of God. It is an honor to call you friend, my dear professor.

Finally, I thank the many pastors and colleagues whom I have had the privilege of working alongside in the trenches. Thank you for your prayers, encouragement, and nods of approval. You reminded me that this message matters. Any clarity in these pages is by God's grace; any shortcomings are mine alone.

Foreword

I CAME TO BE a Jesus follower in the fall of 1968, my junior year in college and smack dab in the middle of the Jesus Movement. In so many ways, it was a wonderful time: leading someone to Christ was like picking apples from the proverbial tree; Christian fellowship was rich and deep; people's lives were changed; the outpouring of new and excellent Christian music was so good that to this day, we as Evangelicals continue to vitalize worship with great Christian music.

There was just one problem, and it is an even bigger problem that most Christians then and now do not know it is a problem: the type of Christianity promulgated was anti-intellectual to its core. Decades ago, church historian Richard Lovelace—an expert on revivals—noted that if a revival occurs, it doesn't last very long unless it is accompanied by a renewal of Christian thinking and the churchwide adoption of this as a core value. I have spoken in hundreds of churches over the last fifty-seven years, and I can say with confidence that such a renewal has not happened. One result is that our culture is progressively slouching towards secular progressiveness according to which Christianity is an outdated superstition "based" on blind faith and emotion. It cannot be taken seriously and, consequently, must be regarded as nothing more than a hobby.

I am committed to the local church and to solid parachurch ministries. So, let us consider the following claim. In an important interview in *Leadership Journal*, Barna Group President David Kinnaman lists six reasons young people leave the church. Four are especially relevant to our current discussion: the church's shallowness of thought, including its biblical teachings and practices; the feeling that it is an unsafe place to express doubts and get answers to questions; its isolationism, that is, its failure to interact fairly with the surrounding culture; and, last but not least, the

FOREWORD

church's anti-science attitude, including being out of step with scientific developments and debate.[1]

What this indicates is that the local church may—I say *may*—do a fair job of teaching people what to believe, but it fails dismally at teaching folks why we should believe. This is absolutely heartbreaking. And it is ironic. Why? Because there has never been a time in the last few centuries when (1) the evidence for God's existence and the truth of Christianity has been so rich and solid, and (2) there are available several books, podcasts, and apologetical ministries of high quality and accessibility. What can be done to change this dire situation?

Here is where Pastor Steve Johnson's book *Stockdale Paradox Christianity* comes in. His main purpose is to awaken people to the current situation to which I have mentioned, to provide a threefold solution to the crisis of our age, and to equip and give courage to people to make a difference for God's kingdom. To be honest, I am overjoyed about this book. It is unique, powerful, accessible, and very interesting. Also, there are so few works about the state of the culture and church that Johnson's book stands out as a must-read. I urge my brothers and sisters to read this work carefully and multiply your efforts by urging others to read it or forming groups to study it. May this book spark the revolution to which Johnson aspires in writing it.

J. P. Moreland
Distinguished Professor of Philosophy
Talbot School of Theology, Biola University

1. Kinnaman, "Six Reasons."

Introduction

THERE IS A STORY that haunts our present moment: a frog, placed in a pot of water, remains still as the temperature slowly rises. Unaware of the danger, it never leaps to safety. It dies, boiled not by the heat alone but by its failure to recognize the slow and subtle change.

That frog is the American church.

Many pastors, elders, and congregants are sitting in pews of comfort while the cultural temperature around them climbs. The pot is no longer warming—it is near boiling. And still, we sing louder, preach softer, and smile politely as the values of Babylon are baptized from our pulpits. The church, once a prophetic voice, now often sounds like an echo of the world it was sent to redeem.

John West, in *Stockholm Syndrome Christianity*,[1] exposes the sinister shift with piercing clarity. He names names and recounts churches and institutions, including his former university, that have quietly handed over their theological birthright for cultural relevance. In their desire not to offend, many have recast sin as merely a different "lifestyle expression." But West sees it for what it is: capitulation. Capture. A spiritual hijacking.

A year prior, Megan Basham's *Shepherds for Sale: How Evangelical Leaders Traded the Truth for a Leftist Agenda*[2] sounded a similar alarm. She chronicled how influential evangelical voices have bartered doctrinal clarity for progressive acceptance. Together, these authors issue a clarion call: we are losing our identity, not because we've been conquered but because we've consented.

This isn't theoretical. On June 3, 2025, on *The Dinesh D'Souza Podcast*, William Wolfe, founder of the Center for Baptist Leadership, warned of progressive infiltration in the Southern Baptist Convention, funded and

---

1. West, *Stockholm Syndrome Christianity*.
2. Basham, *Shepherds for Sale*.

INTRODUCTION

influenced by secular ideologues like George Soros. Wolfe's appeal is not political—it's pastoral. He's urging churches to wake up, stand firm, and remember who we are.³

But the question remains: *Is anyone listening?*

GHOSTING: A SPIRITUAL DIAGNOSIS

For those unfamiliar, Stockholm syndrome refers to a psychological condition in which hostages begin to identify with their captors. Over time, they defend their oppressors and reject rescue. What begins as survival becomes allegiance. What begins as fear becomes fascination. In time, hostages begin to speak well of those who once brutalized them.

Now consider this: the church, once taken "captive" by culture through intimidation, mockery, and marginalization, now aligns with that very culture. We don't simply adopt its language—we celebrate it. We don't just tolerate its idols—we install them on our stages, dress them up with lights, and call it relevance. We don't just explain away its sin—we rebrand it as virtue, applauding what God condemns and condemning what God affirms. Like hostages who've forgotten they were taken, many believers now defend the very ideologies that first sought to destroy them.

This is "Ghosting the Spirit." We keep up the appearances of religion with our services, slogans, and structures, yet we ignore his promptings, sideline his power, and politely decline his interruption. It is spiritual betrayal masked as faithfulness. We scroll past the Spirit's promptings as if they were just another notification, marking them as "read" but leaving them unanswered. Outwardly we sing the songs, but inwardly we have blocked his number, silencing the very One who gives life.

THE STOCKDALE PARADOX: FACING REALITY WITHOUT LOSING HOPE

There is another way—a model not of surrender, but of unyielding courage and brutal honesty. It comes from Vice Admiral James Stockdale, the highest ranking US military officer held captive in the infamous "Hanoi Hilton" during the Vietnam War. Tortured more than twenty times in seven years, Stockdale endured by embracing two truths that most would think

---

3. D'Souza, "Islam and Democracy."

contradictory. On the one hand, he looked his circumstances in the face without flinching, naming the brutal facts of confinement and torment for exactly what they were. On the other hand, he held an immovable confidence that he would ultimately prevail.

This paradox, clear-eyed realism joined to unshakable hope, was not theory for Stockdale; it was the lifeline that kept him alive. And it is precisely this posture the church needs today. Not despair. Not denial. But gritty, grounded hope that stares our cultural captivity in the face and refuses to surrender. Such hope requires clarity about what's broken, courage to reclaim what's worth saving, and resolve to act with Spirit-empowered faith.

FROM DISSERTATION TO DECLARATION

This vision of a Spirit-empowered church on the move is not just abstract to me; it has been the beating heart of my own journey. Nearly two decades ago, I first heard J. P. Moreland speak at a church in Southern California, the very year he released *Kingdom Triangle*. His words stirred me deeply. They were at once simple and profound, and I knew he was putting language to what the Spirit was already inspiring in me. I bought the book, then the audiobook, and went through them a dozen times.

Years later, when I was searching for a doctoral program, I discovered that J. P. was co-leading a cohort called "Engaging Mind and Culture" at Talbot School of Theology. It combined apologetics, ethics, and the integration of the Christian mind as tools for engaging culture. I was all in. I knew from the beginning of the program, without hesitation, what my dissertation had to be: "The Kingdom Triangle as a Manifesto for Personal and Cultural Transformation."

When the day came to defend my 250-page research paper, I sat across from J. P. and Dr. Scott Smith. Both had copies of my dissertation in front of them, yet neither opened it. Instead, they spent forty-five minutes urging me to publish.

Nearly another decade passed before the Spirit pressed that moment back into my soul. This time it was triggered by John West's *Stockholm Syndrome Christianity*. His book compellingly exposed the church's cultural capitulation—but it stopped short. West never pointed to the presence and power of the Holy Spirit as the antidote. As I closed his book, I sensed the Spirit's whisper: "It's time." My dissertation came alive again. What had once been research now became mandate. The Kingdom Triangle was not

Introduction

only a framework; it was the answer to Stockholm capitulation and the way the Spirit longs to ignite his church. This book is the result of that divine compulsion.

WHERE THIS BOOK WILL TAKE YOU

Section One: Crisis of Capitulation

This first section pulls back the curtain on how we arrived at this precarious moment. It names the cultural ideologies that have infiltrated the church, the compromises that have silenced once-bold pulpits, and the slow erosion of conviction disguised as compassion. You will see how small concessions accumulated into sweeping capitulation.

This is not persecution driving us underground; it is surrender by choice. The alarms are ringing, but too many churches are hitting the snooze button. This section is a wake-up call to leaders and members alike: unless we confront the reality of our drift, we will slide further into irrelevance and powerlessness.

Section Two: Kingdom Triangle Algorithm

The second section returns us to the bedrock of kingdom truth. Here we rediscover the simple yet profound framework of J. P. Moreland's *Kingdom Triangle*: life in the Spirit, the renewal of the Christian mind, and the restoration of the Shalom Soul. Together, these three vertices form the framework of renewal, the steady base from which the church advances with power to crash the gates and rescue the captives.

We will examine how biblical authority must be reclaimed, how spiritual gifts must be affirmed, how the mind must be renovated, and how the soul must be restored. This is not optional. Before we can mount a faithful resistance, we must recover what we have neglected: the presence of God, the power of truth, and the courage to think biblically in an age of confusion.

Section Three: Crashing the Gates—Rescuing the Captives

The final section equips believers to move from diagnosis to action. This is where theology becomes movement and conviction becomes courage.

Introduction

You will see what it means to preach truth without apology, disciple the next generation with faithfulness, and stand boldly in public witness when silence feels safer. This is the Spirit-empowered life in motion—forward, united, unstoppable.

Like a crash of rhinoceroses thundering ahead, we may only see thirty feet in front of us, but we follow the One who sees the end from the beginning. Even with limited vision, we move with confidence, knowing that when we charge together in step with the Spirit, the gates of hell cannot withstand the advance. And in a day when many bend the knee to cultural idols, this section calls the church to stand while others bow.

THE DANGER OF GOOD ENOUGH

Before we dive into the chapters ahead, let me share one final moment, one that didn't come from a pulpit or a leadership conference, but from a classroom full of Christian university students.

I was teaching a course on Christian ethics. Most of the students were seniors. Business majors. They weren't there to learn—they were there to get by. Many hadn't turned in assignments. Some plagiarized. Others begged for last-minute mercy. I'll never forget the moment one student pleaded, "Can't you just help me pass?"

That phrase stuck with me: *just passing*. It wasn't just a grade—it was a mindset.

And that's the real issue facing the church today.

We are surrounded by believers who are satisfied with a spiritual D–, who believe that grace means never having to grow. They attend just enough to not feel guilty. Serve just enough to not get questioned. Give just enough to not feel selfish. But friends, the cross was never about just passing. And Jesus didn't endure the agony of Calvary to produce a crowd of average, semi-committed fans. He called disciples. Cross-carriers. Kingdom builders.

Which brings us to a searing insight from Jim Collins in his bestseller, *Good to Great*—one that stings with relevance for the church—*"Good is the enemy of great."*[4]

Most churches don't fail because they're heretical. They fail because they're satisfied. Satisfied with "good" sermons, "good" attendance, "good" programs. But good, in this case, is not good enough—it is the obstacle.

---

4. The title of the first chapter of Collins, *Good to Great*.

Introduction

When church becomes a brand to manage and an audience to entertain, pastors stop being shepherds and start acting like cruise directors, offering family-friendly options to keep the passengers smiling.

But Jesus never said, "Just be good." He said, "Be perfect... as your heavenly Father is perfect" (Matt 5:48). That perfection isn't about being flawless; it's about being fully formed in him.

Not a greatness we achieve, but one we receive as we surrender.
Not perfection through performance, but through abiding.
Not famous, but faithful.
Not polished, but powerful.
The great life is the Spirit-filled life.
The great church is the Spirit-directed church.
It's what we were made for.

So if you're tired of just passing, if you've grown weary of "good enough" Christianity, if you believe Jesus deserves more than a polite nod or a Sunday routine... then turn the page.

Let's leave behind mediocrity in his name and embrace the greatness he empowers.

Not through self-effort. But through Spirit-filled transformation.
Not for applause. But for his glory.
This isn't hype. It's holiness. And it's worth everything.

SECTION ONE

Crisis of Capitulation

In every generation, the church faces its own kind of crisis—a cultural moment that demands clarity, courage, and conviction. But not every generation answers the call. Sometimes, the people of God blink. They trade the dangerous path of discipleship for the comfortable couch of cultural accommodation. This is one of those moments.

Today, we face a crisis not of persecution or external threat but of capitulation—a subtle, insidious surrender to the spirit of the age. What we are witnessing is not merely decline in attendance or the erosion of moral influence. Those are symptoms. The deeper issue is surrender: a surrender of the Christian mind, a surrender of biblical authority, a surrender of missional identity. We've been seduced into believing that relevance requires compromise, that love demands silence, and that faith must be rebranded as "spirituality" to survive in the public square.

But we were never called to survive. We were called to be salt and light—to stand, to speak, to shine. Instead, much of modern Christianity has settled into a kind of spiritual Stockholm Syndrome, identifying more with their captors than the Liberator. Like prisoners who defend their chains, many churches now rush to accommodate the very ideologies that threaten the gospel itself. The result is a compromised church that has lost its prophetic voice. It has become just another echo in the culture's chamber.

The pages that follow are heavy, unflinching, and urgent. They name the brutal facts of our moment: a church seduced by comfort, diluted by compromise, and silenced by fear. Yet, this diagnosis is not the end of the story—it is the beginning. To embrace the hope and renewal that await, we must first understand the depth of our challenge. Without grasping the problem, the good news lacks its power.

This section is a prophetic wake-up call. It confronts the ways we've drifted from our calling, ceded our voice, and softened our witness. The three chapters ahead—"Cultural Drift," "Not the Way It's Supposed to Be," and "Ghosted: Silence of the Shepherds"—lay bare the realities of a faith under siege from within. They are not easy to read. You may feel convicted, unsettled, or even tempted to close the book. I ask you to press on. The truth, though painful, is the foundation for revival.

Chapter 1, "Cultural Drift," reveals how the church has been seduced by a culture that values comfort over conviction. This chapter exposes the subtle shift toward a watered-down faith that prioritizes personal happiness and social acceptance over the gospel's transformative call. It examines how relativism and pragmatism have eroded biblical authority, luring believers into a "just be nice" theology that avoids hard truths.

Chapter 2, "Not the Way It's Supposed to Be," goes deeper into the tectonic shifts beneath the surface. This isn't merely about failing churches or broken institutions. It's about worldview erosion—the loss of a Christian vision of reality that once animated everything from education and politics to art and family. Here we trace how the church abdicated its responsibility to cultivate the life of the mind, ceded authority to secular narratives, and stopped believing that God's truth has something to say about every domain of life. It's a painful reckoning, but one we must not avoid.

Then, in chapter 3, "Ghosted: Silence of the Shepherds," we confront the complicity of Christian leadership in this capitulation. While wolves have always prowled at the edge of the flock, this generation's greater threat may come from within—pastors who remain silent for fear of controversy, or worse, who preach a gospel so diluted it no longer offends anyone. Here, we refuse to blame the culture for what is fundamentally a failure of nerve among those called to guard the truth, speak the word, and equip the saints for battle. This is not condemnation—it is a call to repentance and courage.

These chapters are not the final word—they are the opening argument. "Crisis of Capitulation" names the problem with clarity and urgency, but it does so to prepare the way for solutions. As you read, let the weight of these truths stir you to action. The hope of the gospel shines brightest against the backdrop of reality, and the Lord is calling his people to rise. Return to him. Rend your hearts (Joel 2:12–13). Choose this day whom you will serve (Josh 24:15).

Section One: Crisis of Capitulation

This section, "Crisis of Capitulation," exists to name the brutal facts without flinching. The church is not called to blend in. It is called to break through. And it is only when we recognize the crisis that we can begin to rise from it. Let's begin . . .

CHAPTER 1

Cultural Drift

The greatest danger to the church today is not persecution from the world, but seduction by it.

—Vance Havner, *Havner Devotional Treasury*

The modern church is not being destroyed—it is being digested. Slowly. Almost imperceptibly. Not by open assault, but by accommodation. Not by martyrdom, but by marketing. In her attempt to stay relevant, she has made herself irrelevant. While the early church turned the world upside down, much of the contemporary church has been turned inside out, gutted by compromise and dressed in cultural camouflage. We are no longer prophets crying out in the wilderness; we are promoters curating an experience.

TRADING TRUTH FOR TREND

We have abandoned biblical authority in favor of emotional resonance. Preaching has been replaced by storytelling. Conviction replaced by affirmation. Sanctification by self-help. The sacred has been stripped for parts and sold off in bite-sized, algorithm-friendly pieces—sermon reels, TikTok testimonies, and fashioned spirituality all dressed in the language of "authenticity," yet hollowed out of holiness. This is not revival. It's regression in designer clothes.

Consider the rise and fall of Carl Lentz. His story reads like a modern-day parable, a tale of charisma eclipsing conviction. As the lead pastor of

Hillsong NYC, Lentz didn't just lead a church, he showcased a brand. With his Hollywood jawline, designer wardrobe, and celebrity friendships, he became the poster child for trend-driven Christianity. He baptized Justin Bieber in a luxury penthouse pool and was often seen courtside with NBA stars, seamlessly blending pop culture with pulpit presence.

But beneath the image was a slow erosion of substance. On national platforms, Lentz dodged clear questions about sin, hell, and salvation with vague platitudes and polished deflections. He preached a gospel palatable to the masses but porous to the truth. It wasn't long before moral failure followed, an affair that shocked the faithful but surprised few who had watched the slow drift.[1]

Like Peter, whom Jesus warned that Satan desired to "sift like wheat" (Luke 22:31), Lentz was ensnared by cultural seduction, his compromise wounding the kingdom's witness, leaving broken trust and disillusioned believers. Yet, in God's grace, his story continues. Through repentance, therapy, and sobriety, Lentz has sought family restoration, now serving humbly in a non-pastoral role, aiding recovery programs.[2]

This redemption offers hope to those wrestling with failure, yet the scars of drift remind us: when we chase the applause of men over God's whisper, the gospel's transformative power fades.

This story isn't isolated; it's emblematic. A warning to every church, pastor, and believer: we cannot dress up compromise and call it influence. We cannot exchange holiness for hype. The crowd may cheer, but heaven may weep. And what good is a trending gospel if it has lost its power to transform?

Lentz's drift reflects a broader trend, what Dick Staub aptly calls "Christianity Lite," a faith shaped by cultural comfort rather than costly conviction. This diluted gospel, stripped of repentance and power, leaves us vulnerable to the seduction that ensnared Lentz.

CHRISTIANITY LITE: TASTES GREAT . . . LESS FILLING

Dick Staub named it clearly—"Christianity Lite."[3] It's the kind of faith that appeals to the masses because it costs nothing: no cross, no repentance, no demand for transformation. Just a comfortable Jesus who fits neatly into

1. *The View*, "Hillsong Church Pastor."
2. Lentz, "Carl and Laura Lentz."
3. Staub, *Culturally Savvy Christian*, 18.

our political tribe, affirms our lifestyle choices, and winks at our sins. This Jesus is palatable, portable, and ultimately powerless. He has been declawed and domesticated.

This "Lite" version of Christianity doesn't nourish the soul or renew the mind. It's spiritual aspartame: sweet on the tongue, toxic over time. We have become theological consumers rather than spiritual warriors, more interested in vibe than virtue, more aligned with influencers than intercessors.

Many pulpits have become podiums for cultural conformity. Seminaries have become centers for deconstruction rather than discipleship. The result is a generation of leaders who are fluent in cultural exegesis but biblically illiterate. They are taught how to brand themselves, not how to carry their cross.

What began as a missional attempt to reach the world has turned into a codependent need to be liked by it. We have traded the prophetic for the popular. We are not being persecuted because we are not preaching anything worth persecuting.

....

We are not being persecuted because we are not preaching anything worth persecuting. The gospel is not just good news—it is offensive news. It exposes sin, confronts idols, and announces a kingdom that overthrows the dominion of darkness.

....

We have forgotten that the gospel is not just good news—it is offensive news. It exposes sin. It confronts idols. It announces a kingdom that overthrows the dominion of darkness. But such a gospel will not thrive in a culture of comfort. It must be carried by a church with courage.

THE DRIFT IS NOT ACCIDENTAL

This drift didn't happen overnight. It has come through a thousand small concessions that, taken together, reshaped the very identity of the church. It happened when we began to measure success by attendance instead of allegiance. The numbers on a Sunday morning became more important than the names written in the Lamb's book of life.

It happened when the altar, once a place of tears, repentance, and consecration, was quietly replaced by the auditorium. Pews and prayer benches gave way to theater seats. The architecture itself began to signal that we had shifted from a house of prayer to a house of performance. I remember one church that celebrated tearing out its altars for "better stage visibility." The message was unmistakable: encounter was expendable, but production was not.

It happened when our preaching shifted from declaring eternal truth to soothing felt needs. Sermons became self-help pep talks: practical, polished, even inspiring, but too often stripped of the call to repentance or the fire of the Spirit. People left affirmed but not transformed, comforted but not convicted.

And it happened when the church found it easier to say *yes* to culture while offering only a timid *maybe* to Christ. Whether on issues of morality, sexuality, or truth itself, the church often adopted the world's language, hoping relevance would win respect. But each *yes* to culture was, in practice, a *no* to the cross.

None of these choices seemed catastrophic in the moment. They were defended as practical, relevant, or compassionate. But over time, they added up. Together they have carried us not into cultural strength, but to the edge of spiritual irrelevance. The great crisis of our age is not that culture has become too strong, but that the church has become too soft.

THE CRISIS BEFORE US

This is the crisis of capitulation. And it's not hypothetical. It's happening in real time, in our worship sets, in our youth ministries, in our pulpits, and in our silence on moral issues that demand a prophetic voice. Nowhere is this more evident than in the unfolding fracture within the United Methodist Church—a denomination once known for its evangelical fervor and scriptural faithfulness.

In 2024, the United Methodist Church officially dismantled its longstanding doctrinal boundaries on human sexuality. At the denomination's General Conference in Charlotte, delegates voted by overwhelming margins to delete all restrictive language regarding homosexuality from the *Book of Discipline*—including the pivotal paragraph 304.3, which for nearly five decades had declared, "The practice of homosexuality is incompatible with Christian teaching. Therefore, self-avowed practicing homosexuals are not to be certified as candidates, ordained as ministers, or appointed to serve in The United Methodist Church."[4] This line had stood as the moral spine of Methodist orthodoxy since 1972. Its removal in 2024 marked a watershed moment, effectively reversing the denomination's biblical stance and signaling a theological retreat from clarity to accommodation.

The deletions went far beyond a single paragraph. The 2024 revisions struck multiple disciplinary prohibitions: clergy may now officiate same-sex weddings without penalty, and conferences are free to ordain non-celibate LGBTQ clergy. Restrictions once forbidding the use of church funds to "promote the acceptance of homosexuality" were erased as well. The UMC's own official explainer confirmed:

> Much of what was deleted are former prohibitions involving homosexual people . . . including prohibitions against self-avowed, practicing homosexual persons serving as clergy . . . and against clergy presiding at same-sex weddings.[5]

What replaced these clear prohibitions were broad, noncommittal affirmations. The revised *Book of Discipline* now reads, "The United Methodist Church acknowledges that all persons are of sacred worth"[6] and that "human sexuality [is] a sacred gift"[7] while redefining marriage as "a sacred, lifelong covenant that brings together two people of faith, or two adult persons . . . of consenting age."[8] Even denominational leaders described the goal as a move toward neutrality, explaining that the changes were intended "to bring the *Book of Discipline* back to a neutral place . . . holding space for differing opinions within The United Methodist Church by avoiding broad mandates."[9]

But neutrality is never neutral. By trading conviction for consensus, the UMC has not found balance—it has surrendered biblical ground. Where once this Church drew its compass from Scripture, it now orients itself by culture. The rhetoric of inclusion has become the theology of dilution. What was once a Wesleyan movement of revival has become a monument to relativism. This is not reform—it is regression. It is Stockholm Christianity: a denomination held hostage by the very ideologies it

---

4. The United Methodist Church, *Book of Discipline* (2016), para. 304.3.
5. Burton Edwards, "Human Sexuality."
6. The United Methodist Church, *Book of Discipline* (2024), para. 4.
7. The United Methodist Church, *Book of Discipline* (2024), para. 162.C.
8. The United Methodist Church, *Book of Discipline* (2024), para. 162.D.
9. The United Methodist Church, "Understanding General Conference 2024."

was called to confront, confusing compassion with compromise and mercy with moral amnesia.

MIRROR OF THE CULTURE: THE DEVOLUTION OF SACRED IDENTITY

The church was once known for her distinctiveness—a radiant city on a hill, a community that refused to be assimilated into the culture around her. But now, in many corners of the Western world, she has become a hall of mirrors, reflecting back to the world its own broken image with a faint halo of spiritual language.

The language of the sanctuary now echoes the slogans of the street. "Live your truth." "Be true to yourself." "God just wants you to be happy." These are not the words of Christ, they are the mantras of Moral Therapeutic Deism,[10] the default religion of the West, where God is a divine butler, Jesus is a life coach, and sin is nothing more than a bad vibe.

It is a pseudoreligion that reduces God to a divine therapist, Jesus to an affirming sidekick, and holiness to the pursuit of personal happiness. We do not confront the culture; we confirm it. We don't transform minds; we cater to moods. Somewhere along the line, sacred identity was exchanged for cultural validation.

This was not merely a tactical error—it was a theological collapse. Rooted in the drift toward postmodern relativism, the church has increasingly come to define truth not by revelation, but by resonance. If it feels good, if it sounds positive, if it garners clicks, then it must be righteous. This is the air we breathe: vague spirituality, therapeutic positivity, and ethical elasticity. The problem is not that the world has become post-Christian, it's that the church has become post-biblical.

Many modern churches boast of being "safe spaces" where no one will feel judged—but they have forgotten that the gospel is not safe. It is a sword, not a suggestion. It is liberation, but only through confrontation. The early church preached with conviction because they knew the world was at war with truth. Today, we whisper affirmations because we are unsure whether truth even exists.

This collapse of sacred identity is not accidental. It's the predictable result of a church that sought relevance by sacrificing reverence. And when reverence is lost, so is power.

10. Smith and Lundquist Denton, *Soul Searching*, 162–63.

Cultural Drift

A vivid example of this collapse can be seen in the rise and fall of Mars Hill Church in Seattle. Founded by Mark Driscoll, Mars Hill grew rapidly, attracting thousands of young adults with its edgy presentation, cultural savvy, and strong personality leadership. While the church proclaimed biblical truth, its tone often mirrored the very aggression, celebrity obsession, and platform-driven culture it sought to critique. Over time, the theological depth was eclipsed by a toxic leadership culture, authoritarian control, and a steady slide into brand over body.

In 2014, following multiple investigations into abuse of power and spiritual bullying, Mark Driscoll resigned from Mars Hill Church, and within months, the entire multicampus network disbanded amid widespread fallout. The wreckage was massive, with former members grappling with betrayal and loss of community. One ex-attendee reflected, "I came for Jesus, but Mark's intensity kept me hooked—until the bullying and control made it untenable."[11]

The fall of Mars Hill was not only a leadership failure but also the collapse of a model that prioritized visibility over vitality, sacrificing sacred identity for market relevance and leaving many believers disillusioned, questioning whether it was ever truly a church.

When the church mirrors the culture instead of modeling the kingdom, it may gain an audience—but it loses its anointing.

THE MIRACULOUS WAS THE NORM

Examples of this drift are everywhere. The Foursquare denomination, founded by Aimee Semple McPherson in the 1920s, was once ablaze with the supernatural. McPherson herself was known for dramatic healings, Holy Spirit–empowered preaching, and bold declarations of faith. Her Angelus Temple in Los Angeles saw thousands flock nightly during the Depression era, seeking divine intervention. The denomination's early years were marked by revival tents, deliverances, and altar calls filled with weeping saints.

However, in more recent decades, many Foursquare congregations have slowly moved away from active pursuit of the charisms. A 2014 report from the Foursquare Church encouraged local congregations to emphasize "contextual mission" and "community relevance."[12] While these aims

---

11. Johnson, *Rise and Fall*, 202.
12. Burris, "Important Reimagine Discussions."

are not inherently problematic, they reflect a broader trend away from the supernatural distinctives that once defined the movement.

Glenn Burris Jr., then-president of the denomination at the time, emphasized the importance of seeking the Spirit's power alongside strategies for community engagement. Yet in practice, many churches have settled for clever programming over charismatic power. The consequence is a spiritual dulling, where the expectancy for the miraculous is lost, even if doctrinally affirmed.

A similar drift has occurred within many Calvary Chapel fellowships. Born out of the Jesus Movement of the 1960s and 1970s, Calvary Chapel was known for its openness to the supernatural, with founder Chuck Smith emphasizing spontaneous baptisms, the gifts of the Spirit, and a posture of expectation toward the miraculous. Smith's oft-repeated phrase, "I don't believe in a powerless gospel," captured the theological heartbeat of a movement that valued both expositional teaching and Spirit-led ministry.

However, following Smith's death in 2013, a noticeable shift began to emerge across many Calvary Chapel congregations. While the denomination continues to affirm the present-day ministry of the Holy Spirit, in practice, the experiential dimension of worship has diminished. Many younger pastors within the movement have embraced a more cautious, Reformed orientation—trading the vibrancy of Spirit-led spontaneity for the stability of expositional certainty. Worship services have become more scripted, altar ministry more restrained, and the gifts of the Spirit more assumed than expected.

This recalibration is perhaps most publicly symbolized by Greg Laurie—one of Calvary Chapel's most visible leaders—who formally aligned his church with the Southern Baptist Convention. While still preaching a gospel of salvation, Laurie's shift illustrates a broader theological drift: from charismatic openness to institutional conservatism. In many churches that once hosted afterglows and healing prayer, the gifts are no longer pursued with urgency but remembered with nostalgia.

The drift wasn't announced with fanfare, but its effects are evident. Calvary Chapel was once marked by a holy tension between word and Spirit—a commitment to biblical depth and supernatural vitality. But in many places, that tension has relaxed into predictability. The fire hasn't gone out entirely, but it burns lower, dimmed by a desire to be safe, structured, and sensible.[13]

---

13. For more, see Shellnut, "Tale of Two Calvary Chapels."

Even the Assemblies of God, one of the world's largest Pentecostal denominations, has shown signs of internal tension. While the national office continues to affirm Pentecostal doctrine, local expressions vary widely across the movement. Some congregations still embrace extended altar ministry and the gifts of the Spirit, but many have drifted toward structured services with dimmed lights, countdown clocks, and sermons shaped more by cultural resonance than by Spirit-empowered urgency.

As someone who has been ordained with the Assemblies of God for over thirty years, serving on staff and speaking in countless AG churches, I can say this with firsthand clarity: the overwhelming majority no longer promote the Pentecostal distinctives that once defined us. Altar calls are abbreviated or nonexistent. Gifts are referenced in theory but rarely practiced in the sanctuary. The result? A movement in danger of maintaining a Pentecostal name while shedding its Pentecostal power.

This concern was echoed in 2011 by former General Superintendent George O. Wood, who warned of Pentecostals becoming "practical cessationists"—believers in the baptism of the Holy Spirit who fail to practice, expect, or experience it in daily life. If we lose our fire, we lose our identity. His statement was not hyperbole; it was a prophetic diagnosis urging a return to Pentecostal roots.[14]

The supernatural didn't cease—our appetite did. What was once expected is now optional. What was once pursued is now programmed.

STOCKHOLM SYNDROME CHRISTIANITY

When a person is held captive long enough, something strange can happen: the captive begins to sympathize with the captor. Psychologists call it Stockholm Syndrome: a survival mechanism where hostages develop loyalty to those who oppress them. In exchange for protection, identity, or perceived favor, they begin to defend the very structures that enslave them. John West did a magnificent job explaining this and naming churches and pastors that have bought into the capitulation.[15]

It is no longer a clinical phenomenon. It has become a theological one. The modern church is showing all the signs of Stockholm Syndrome Christianity, not merely oppressed by cultural ideologies but enamored with them. We have so absorbed the language, logic, and loves of the dominant

14. Wood, "Pentecost."
15. West, *Stockholm Syndrome Christianity*.

culture that we now instinctively defend what we once denounced. We have become apologists for our captors, explaining away their abuses in the name of empathy, dialogue, and "nuance."

This shift is a willful dissociation from the apostolic imagination. That is, the church no longer sees herself as a Spirit-empowered resistance movement, but as a managed religious brand seeking social credibility. Instead of confronting Babylon, she has moved in and redecorated.

We now affirm what culture celebrates and stay silent where culture rages. And when true prophets speak, we distance ourselves from them. We label them divisive. Harsh. Unwise. We rush to clarify, to contextualize, to soften the sting. But the reality is this: we are afraid. Afraid of cultural rejection. Afraid of being misunderstood. Afraid of losing our seat at a table Jesus never asked us to sit at.

Like captives too long in the dungeon of compromise, we have grown accustomed to the dark. Instead of standing firm in our faith, we've started to embrace the very ideas that challenge it:

- We let the world's views on who we are overshadow the truth that we're made in God's image.
- We buy into cultural arguments that make justice and truth seem like opposites, as if living righteously means abandoning God's word.
- We settle for a self-focused faith that treats discipleship like personal wellness, calling it spiritual growth when it's just comfort in disguise.

This is not Christian compassion. It is Christian captivity. Stockholm Christians are quick to rebuke their own prophets but slow to question their cultural priests. They share more quotes from Brené Brown and Deepak Chopra than from Jeremiah. They are scandalized by dogma but soothed by self-actualization. And tragically, they believe they are being "like Jesus"—not realizing they have become like Pilate, trying to keep the peace while washing their hands of responsibility.

This captivity has a spiritual cost. The more we accommodate our captors, the more we grieve the Spirit who empowers the church to stand in contrast, not in agreement. But this isn't new. The people of God have been here before.

Cultural Drift

THE DEUTERONOMIC WARNINGS: ANCIENT DRIFT, MODERN ECHO

The crisis we now face is not novel—it is covenantal. What the modern church is experiencing is not just a cultural decline but a spiritual déjà vu. We have been here before. The Bible has a word for this moment, and it is not ignorance—it is forgetfulness.

The book of Deuteronomy, Moses' final address to the people of Israel, rings with urgency. The promised land was within reach, but so was spiritual amnesia. Over and over, Yahweh warns his people not to forget. Not to dilute. Not to mix devotion with convenience. Because the greatest threat to their faith wasn't external persecution—it was internal erosion. "Be careful that you don't forget the LORD your God by failing to keep His command" (Deut 8:11).

This was not a mild concern. It was a prophetic fire alarm. Moses foresaw what prosperity, peace, and cultural integration would do to the people of God if they lost their awe of him. He warned that if they traded exclusive allegiance to Yahweh for syncretistic security, they would not only lose their mission, they would lose their identity. "When you eat and are full, and build beautiful houses to live in, ... and everything else you have increases, be careful that your heart doesn't become proud and you forget the LORD your God" (Deut 8:12–14).

Sound familiar?

Today, we too live in comfort, abundance, and the trappings of platforms, buildings, and strategies. And like Israel, we are tempted to believe that success is the same as favor. But God's covenant is not sustained by trends, it is sustained by obedience. And obedience always requires exclusive loyalty. "Do not follow other gods, the gods of the peoples around you, for the LORD your God, ... among you, is a jealous God" (Deut 6:14–15).

The American church, like ancient Israel, has not so much rejected God as it has replaced him. Not with Baal or Asherah, but with relevance, affirmation, control, and safety. And like Israel, we have convinced ourselves that we can worship Yahweh while flirting with the high places.

FROM POWER TO PROGRAM: THE EVANGELICAL SUBSTITUTION

When the glory departed, we didn't repent—we reorganized. Rather than tear our garments in sorrow over the absence of divine power, we tailored new ones in the name of excellence and efficiency. What began as a hunger to reach the lost was subtly hijacked by a need to retain control. We exchanged the unpredictable movement of the Holy Spirit for the predictable mechanics of modern ministry. And in doing so, we created an evangelical ecosystem that runs efficiently—without requiring God.

This is the tragedy of the evangelical substitution: when the presence of God ceased to be the engine of the church, we replaced it with programming. The seeker-sensitive movement, though birthed from sincere evangelistic concern, became the catalyst for a church model obsessed with attraction. Stagecraft replaced supplication. Metrics replaced miracles. The pulpit turned into a platform, and sermons became presentations tailored to spiritual consumers. This wasn't innovation—it was insulation. It shielded us from the wildness of the Spirit.

We stopped waiting in the upper room and started strategizing in the boardroom. The Church Growth Movement, driven by pragmatism rather than pneumatology, created churches that are numerically full but spiritually malnourished. They are engineered to retain crowds, not revive hearts. And as long as the offering flows and the attendance holds, we have learned to live without fire from heaven.[16]

But the question that haunts this moment is not "Does it work?"

It's "Is he with us?"

God's presence is not guaranteed by good intentions or careful planning. In Exod 33, God warned Moses, "I will send an angel ahead of you . . . but I will not go with you" (verses 2–3). That is, the mission would still be accomplished, but without divine presence. Moses' response should be ours: "If Your presence does not go, . . . don't make us go up from here" (Exod 33:15).

Yet much of the modern church has reversed the prayer. We say, "As long as the mission is working, we're good." But we're not. Because if we can grow ministries without holiness, multiply campuses without consecration, and maintain budgets without obedience, we are not in revival—we are in rebellion.

---

16. Newton, "Church Growth."

Cultural Drift

The Spirit is not an optional accessory to our programming. He is the source. Without him, we are not a church—we are a brand. When the miraculous was forfeited, marketing filled the vacuum. When the charisms were discarded, charisma took center stage. When the mandate was ignored, the model became sacred. This is not Spirit-led ministry. It is a management philosophy baptized in Christian language.

But beneath the polish, the lights, and the fog machines, a silent question lingers in the soul of the faithful remnant: Where is the Lord, the God of Elijah? The answer is simple. He is where he has always been: looking for a people who have not bowed to Baal, who are not satisfied with performance, and who long not for relevance but for revival.

Nowhere is this more evident than in the rise of seeker-sensitive churches that prioritize production over presence. Joel Osteen's Lakewood Church fills stadiums, with an average weekly attendance exceeding forty-five thousand and a broadcast audience in the millions. But despite the scale, his sermons famously avoid the discomforts of doctrine—rarely mentioning sin, repentance, or the necessity of the cross. As theologian Michael Horton observes, "Osteen promotes sin as failing to live up to our potential, not falling short of God's glory. . . . In fact, one would be hard-pressed to find anything in this [Osteen's] message that would be offensive to a Unitarian, Buddhist, or cultural Christians who are used to a diet of gospel-as-American-Dream."[17] God's role is reduced to affirming human success, offering a gospel indistinguishable from self-help platitudes. This is not prophecy—it is positivity. And it leaves the soul unchallenged and unchanged.

Similarly, Willow Creek Community Church, once a beacon of innovative church growth, admitted in its 2007 "Reveal" study that decades of strategic programming had failed to produce mature believers. The study's conclusion was stunning: "We made a mistake. We should have taught people how to grow in their relationship with Christ, not just kept them busy in church activities." Bill Hybels confessed publicly, "We built the church on programs and not on spiritual practices."[18]

What both Lakewood and Willow Creek demonstrate is this: activity is not vitality. A full calendar is not the same as a full heart. Production is not presence. We have built systems that can attract crowds but cannot cultivate character.

17. Horton, "Joel Osteen."
18. Hybels, foreword to Hawkins et al., *Reveal*, 4.

STOCKDALE PARADOX CHRISTIANITY

BUCKLEY'S PROPHETIC WORD AND THE EVANGELICAL ELITE

Long before many in the church were ready to admit it, William F. Buckley Jr. saw it. In his blistering critique of the American university system, *God and Man at Yale*, he made a declaration that now reads like a prophetic lament: "Yale is not merely a secular institution, but a determinedly anti-Christian one."[19]

That was 1951. He wasn't writing about a pagan empire—he was indicting an institution founded in covenantal allegiance to Christ. What Buckley observed in the academy has now metastasized in the church. His warning was prophetic—not just for academia but for the church.

What Yale institutionalized, the American evangelical church has now normalized and internalized. The same disease has infected the ecclesial bloodstream. Where once we trained prophets, we now produce pundits. Where once we discipled apostles, we now credential entrepreneurs. The gospel of the kingdom has been domesticated into the gospel of respectability.

Evangelical elite, celebrity pastors, mega-platform authors, thought-leaders addicted to conferences and cameras—they now shape much of the theological atmosphere. And increasingly, they are functionally agnostic about the supernatural. They may not deny miracles explicitly, but their silence is loud. Their models make no room for the unpredictable. Their systems are optimized for scalability, not surrender.

We now have leaders more concerned with offending Facebook or X than grieving the Spirit. The seminaries that once formed preachers to walk in power have become safe spaces for intellectual detachment. To speak of healing, prophecy, or tongues in many theological institutions is to be met with smirks or suspicion. The Spirit is reduced to a doctrinal footnote. Revival is reserved for history books. And the miraculous? That's for "those kinds" of churches.

But make no mistake: this is not caution, it is compromise. It is the theological fruit of what Buckley exposed in the academy: a self-assured, disembodied intellectualism that despises the vibrant immediacy of a Spirit-filled church. And it has made its home in pulpits across the land.

The result? A new priesthood of sophisticated unbelievers in clerical garb: pastors fluent in Greek but foreign to groaning in the Spirit, leaders

---

19. Buckley, *God and Man at Yale*, 26.

who can parse a pericope but cannot cast out demons, influencers who can win a crowd but cannot weep in intercession.

We do not need more evangelical elites. We need Elijahs. We need those who will stand on Carmel, drenched in cultural fire retardant, and cry out, "The God who answers by fire—He is God!" We need preachers who believe the Spirit didn't retire in the first century. We need scholars who tremble at the word of the Lord, not the approval of the guild.

If Buckley's words were true of Yale, how much more indicting are they now of the church? A church that forgets her roots, ignores her mandate, and mocks her inheritance is not enlightened. She is apostate. And if she does not awaken, she will not be opposed by God—she will be abandoned by him (see Rev 3).

SPECTACLE WITHOUT SUBSTANCE: THE CAUTION OF BETHEL

To balance the critique, consider Bethel Church in Redding, California. Bethel embraces signs, wonders, and Spirit-filled ministry but has often been criticized for confusing spectacle with substance.[20] Controversial practices such as gold dust appearing during worship services, claims of angel feathers falling from ceilings, and the highly debated practice of "grave soaking"—where individuals lie on the graves of past revivalists in hopes of absorbing their spiritual anointing—have drawn both fascination and ridicule.[21]

Leaders at Bethel have acknowledged some of these reports while attempting to distance official church doctrine from extremes, such as Bill Johnson clarifying that neither he nor Bethel encourages grave soaking.[22] Pastor Bill Johnson has emphasized pursuing the full realities of God's kingdom, stating, "Seek first the kingdom of God and His righteousness, and all these things shall be added to you," while anchoring faith in Scripture and the unseen realm.[23] Still, many within and outside the Pentecostal world have raised concerns. One analysis notes that "it is Bethel's proximity to the truth that generates confusion within American Christianity."[24]

20. Carter, "9 Things."
21. Carter, "9 Things."
22. Carter, "9 Things."
23. Johnson, *When Heaven Invades Earth*, 41.
24. Kennedy, "Christian Idolatry?"

This is not a condemnation but a caution. The pursuit of the supernatural is vital, but it must actually be tethered to Scripture. Spirit without Scripture leads to wildfire. Scripture without Spirit leads to a frozen wasteland. We are called to burn with both heat and light.

COMPLICITY IN SILENCE: WHEN THE PULPIT BECAME PASSIVE

There was a time when the pulpit was thunder, when prophets trembled before they preached, and congregations wept before they responded. When truth was not a brand strategy but a sacred trust. But now? In far too many places, the pulpit has gone passive. And its silence is not neutral—it is complicit.

Silence in the face of deception is not discretion, it is betrayal. And yet, week after week, pulpits across the Western world echo with carefully crafted messages that avoid controversy, dodge conviction, and cradle the congregation in psychological comfort. We have confused being "seeker-friendly" with being Spirit-empty. We no longer fear God—we fear being unfollowed.

Where is the voice that will speak into the moral madness of our age? Where are the pastors who will name the gods of our culture—sexual autonomy, expressive individualism, ethnic idolatry, consumerism, and political syncretism—and declare without stammer or apology, "You shall have no other gods before Yahweh"?

Instead, many pulpits have become pulp. Soft. Malleable. Flavorless. And in the name of nuance, we've lost our nerve. We are loud where culture affirms us and silent where Scripture confronts it. We do not speak of sin because sin suggests there is something from which we must be saved. We do not speak of judgment because judgment implies there is a Judge. We do not speak of the Spirit's power because power cannot be controlled. And so we speak of leadership, self-improvement, and loving yourself better.

But the silence has a price. It is forming a generation of spiritually anesthetized believers—souls who can quote Christian clichés but have never been broken over their sin, who are affirmed in their dysfunction but never delivered from it.

And behind the silence is strategy. Silence is often disguised as wisdom: "Let's not be political"; "Let's focus on the gospel"; "Let's not alienate anyone." But this is not gospel fidelity—it's gospel avoidance. For the gospel has always been political in the truest sense: it announces a King and a kingdom that confronts every empire and every idol. Jesus wasn't crucified for clever parables. He was crucified because he refused to accommodate. And neither will his true followers.

Capitulation always begins with soft speech when the edge of the prophetic voice is dulled by the fear of man. But the edge must be restored. The pulpit must regain its roar. We are not entertainers. We are not therapists. We are not corporate executives. We are oracles of a holy God, called to stand between the living and the dead and to speak fire.

If the watchman stays silent, blood is on his hands (Ezek 33:6). And if the shepherd refuses to correct, the sheep will be devoured. We are out of time for passive preaching. The church must speak now—or she will be spoken for by forces that know no mercy and recognize no truth.

THE HEBRAIC WARNING: DRIFTING IS DEATH

If the warnings of Deuteronomy revealed the ancient pattern of spiritual erosion, the New Testament reaffirms that the danger did not end with Israel. The writer of Hebrews, addressing a community tempted to compromise under cultural pressure, doesn't mince words: "We must, therefore, pay even more attention to what we have heard, so that we will not drift away" (Heb 2:1).

Drift is a deceptively gentle word. It implies no rebellion, no open denial, no violent schism. It feels like relaxing. You don't notice it until you've lost sight of the shore. It's just a quiet, unhurried departure. Like a boat unmoored, it doesn't resist the current. It simply yields to it.

Drift never announces itself with trumpets. It slips in quietly, concession by concession, until you wake up in a place you never intended to be.

And that is precisely the danger. The church rarely apostatizes overnight. Instead, she forgets to anchor. She loosens her grip on sound doctrine. She becomes tolerant of what she once rejected and bored with what once gave her life. She doesn't charge toward the cliff—she sleepwalks off of it.

The Greek word used here, *pararrhueō*, evokes a slow, silent slipping past a safe harbor. It is not a dramatic leap into apostasy, it is a passive slide into irrelevance. And its result is just as deadly.

PROPHETIC CALL TO RECLAIM THE MANDATE

Let the church remember who she is and reclaim what she abandoned.

Because the mandate remains.

The Spirit still speaks.

And, the Father still waits.

We have drifted far. But how did we get here? If the church is now a shadow of its former calling, we must dig deeper—not just into what we see but into what we've allowed. The next chapter doesn't just name the problem. It begins tracing the slow, intentional slide into spiritual paralysis.

So, we ask the question:

What went wrong? Because this is not the way it was supposed to be.

CHAPTER 2

Not the Way It's Supposed to Be

If I find in myself a desire which no experience in this world can satisfy, the most probable explanation is that I was made for another world.

—C. S. Lewis, *Mere Christianity*

In the opening chapter of Cornelius Plantinga's book *Not the Way It's Supposed to Be*, he cites a powerful scene from the film *Grand Canyon*. Kevin Kline's character, Mack, takes a detour to avoid traffic and ends up broken down in a crime-ridden neighborhood. Before the tow truck arrives, a group of local thugs confronts him. Just as things are about to take a violent turn, Simon, the tow truck driver played by Danny Glover, arrives and immediately begins to hook up the car as he observes something bad is about to go down. He pulls aside the gang leader and says,

> Man, the world ain't supposed to work like this. Maybe you don't know that, but this ain't the way it's supposed to be. I'm supposed to be able to do my job without askin' you if I can. And that dude is supposed to be able to wait with his car without you rippin' him off. Everything's supposed to be different than what it is here.[1]

Plantinga titles his first chapter "Vandalism of Shalom." He describes shalom as universal flourishing, wholeness, and delight: the way things ought to be. By citing this scene, Plantinga drives home the disconnect that plays out across every culture: everything's supposed to be different than

---

1. Kasdan, *Grand Canyon*, 18:45.

what it is. He points out that God hates sin not merely because it breaks his law, but more deeply because it vandalizes shalom. Sin breaks the peace. It violates the design. God is for shalom and therefore against sin.[2]

Plantinga helps us see that this disconnect is not just moral, but teleological—it speaks to purpose and design. Something is malfunctioning in the world. Creation is not operating according to the Manufacturer's specifications. The same can be said for the church. Something is not the way it's supposed to be.

•••••••••••••••••••••••••••••••••••

The fall is not a footnote in history—it is the atmosphere we all inhale. Until we name that reality, healing will remain theoretical and redemption will feel unnecessary.

•••••••••••••••••••••••••••••••••••

LOSING THE PLOT

In any great story, there's a plot—a driving narrative that shapes the actions of its characters. Remove the plot, and the story unravels. The same is true of Christianity. The gospel is not just a set of beliefs or moral code; it is the grand, Spirit-empowered, Christ-centered story of redemption, transformation, and restoration. Yet somewhere along the way, the church lost the plot.

It began in an upper room: cramped, uncertain, electric. A room of waiting, of hunger, of promise. They had no building, no budget, and no branding—only a command: "Stay in the city until you are empowered from on high" (see Luke 24:49). And when it came, it came like fire.

What followed was not a spiritual philosophy, but a living eruption. Power flowed. Lives were changed. Cities stirred. The early church didn't argue people into the kingdom; they turned the world upside down. The presence of the Spirit wasn't a doctrinal footnote; it was the animating force of the Christian life.

To be a Christian was to be Spirit-born, Spirit-filled, Spirit-led.

But what happens when the fire flickers?

---

2. Plantinga, *Not the Way*, 14.

Not the Way It's Supposed to Be

In the early chapters of Acts, we find a vibrant, Spirit-filled movement of disciples who lived with purpose, power, and presence. But in the centuries that followed, that movement often became a monument—an institutionalized version of faith that traded intimacy for influence, power for position, and dynamic transformation for static tradition. We must ask, What went wrong?

This chapter is not an academic exercise in church history. It's a search-and-rescue mission. If the people of God are going to recapture the fullness of kingdom life, we must understand how we veered off course. Only then can we rediscover the path of Spirit-empowered living and reverse the drift.

Let me explain with an illustration. On a recent trip to Austin, my wife and I watched the grandkids while our youngest son and his wife took off for an anniversary getaway. We used his Tesla while we were there. I'd never been in one.

Before they left, my son handed me what looked like a credit card. No keys. I looked at him and asked, "What do I do with this?" He grinned and said, "Just wave it at the door." I did—and the door unlocked.

I looked at him and said, "Seriously?" He nodded. "Now just put the card right here on the pad and buckle up." I placed it on the console, clicked my seat belt, and the whole thing came to life.

It was like climbing into the cockpit of a jet. Everything was silent, smooth, loaded with tech. Driving is driving, sure—but this was in a category all its own.

Later that day, when we got home, Greg asked me to back it into the driveway so he could plug it in. The battery was showing 20 percent. "Gotta charge it," he said. "You'll need the power." That moment stuck with me. Because as advanced and sleek as that Tesla is, as futuristic and loaded as it may be, without power, it's dead. All the features in the world don't matter if it's disconnected from the source. No hum. No movement. No power.

You've got the frame. You've got the form. But you're missing the charge. That, in many ways, has been the story of the church over the past two millennia. The external shape remained. But somewhere along the road, the spiritual voltage dropped. The early believers had fire in their bones. Too often today, we settle for fog machines, special lighting, huge video screens, and clever branding. And we wonder why the engine of transformation no longer roars.

This chapter is not a nostalgic lament for "the good old days," nor is it a call for emotionalism or theological excess. It is a serious reckoning with what has been lost, and what must be regained if we are to fulfill the mission Jesus left us.

We need to look honestly at the long slide from Spirit-powered faith to program-driven religion. From presence-based ministry to personality-driven leadership. From kingdom confrontation to cultural accommodation.

How did we get here? The drift didn't happen in a day. It happened through centuries of compromise—often slow, subtle, and respectable. But it all began with this: we exchanged presence for position. We gained the world's acceptance but lost heaven's power.

THE DRIFT BEGINS

The early church was raw, real, and reliant. They didn't engineer their power—they received it. No one had ever seen anything like it: a marginalized, underresourced community healing the sick, confronting injustice, proclaiming resurrection, and rejoicing in suffering—all with supernatural courage and joy.

But it didn't take long for that unfiltered dependence on the Spirit to be replaced with something safer, more systematized, and socially accepted. The drift didn't begin with rebellion—it began with convenience. The church gained visibility and viability but lost volatility. It became a fixture rather than a force.

FROM UPPER ROOM TO IMPERIAL COURT

The fourth century marked one of the most dramatic turns in church history. Constantine's conversion and the Edict of Milan (AD 313) brought an end to violent persecution. For the first time, the church could breathe. And then, it began to settle.

What had been a grassroots, Spirit-ignited movement began to take on the structure of empire. Bishops gained political clout. Worship was formalized. Church buildings became ornate. The cross moved from blood-stained arenas to gilded altars.

In many ways, this newfound acceptance brought blessings: safety, structure, and widespread influence. But it also created a shift beneath the surface—no longer did the church need power from on high; it now had favor from on earth. The early Christians waited for fire from heaven. The post-Constantinian church learned to build fires on their own.

It's not that faith vanished. But the Spirit was gradually institutionalized—boxed in by liturgy, displaced by politics, and increasingly filtered through hierarchy rather than intimacy

WHEN FAITH BECOMES A FORMALITY

In this new structure, personal transformation was replaced by public tradition. Miracles became rare—or explained away. Augustine of Hippo, one of the church's most influential thinkers, initially claimed signs and wonders had ceased with the apostles.[3] Yet after witnessing deliverance and healing firsthand, he changed his mind.

In *City of God*, Augustine cataloged more than seventy miracles in his lifetime, many tied to prayer and the relics of Saint Stephen. Though cautious in tone, he confessed, "Even now, many miracles are worked . . . but they are not so well known as those which were written . . . for the benefit of the faith of the nations."[4]

Still, the theological trajectory was already shifting. Spirit-empowered living became exceptional instead of expected. Doctrine was elevated. Liturgy was codified. But intimacy with the Spirit drifted to the margins.

The church began to look more like a department of the state than a supernatural body of believers. Discipleship became doctrinal compliance, not divine encounter. The sacraments remained—but their charge was muted.

FROM DEPENDENCE TO DESIGN

This is the subtle seduction of institutional faith: when we learn to operate without the Spirit, we grow confident in our programs, processes, and platforms. We start to trust the machine we've built—forgetting that what once made us dangerous was our dependence.

A Tesla without power is just a beautifully engineered shell. Every curve, every touchscreen, every software update—it's all meaningless without one thing: charge. And unlike gas gauges in traditional vehicles,

---

3. Augustine, *City of God* 22.8.
4. Augustine, *City of God* 22.8 (Bettenson, 1033).

a Tesla doesn't even pretend. Front and center is the battery percentage. That number isn't cosmetic—it tells you exactly how much life, motion, and access you have left. It doesn't matter how brilliant the design is if the battery is at "0" percent. The battery isn't a bonus, it's everything. So it is with the church.

We can carry the name. We can polish the brand. We can upgrade the experience. But if we're not plugged into the Spirit, we may resemble the early church in form, but we lack its fire. No movement. No mission. No miracle.

ENLIGHTENMENT AND THE AGE OF THE EMPTY CHURCH

As the centuries passed, the church's growing reliance on structure was soon reinforced by a cultural shift that would alter the Western world, and the church within it, at its core.

The Enlightenment, often hailed as a triumph of reason, brought many undeniable benefits: scientific advancement, political reform, educational expansion. But it also carried an invisible cost, especially for the church. With reason elevated as the supreme authority, the supernatural, Spirit-infused life was slowly placed on trial. The miraculous, once assumed, now had to be explained—or explained away.

FAITH IN THE AGE OF REASON

The age of faith gave way to the age of facts. Revelation was replaced with rationalism. Instead of "thus saith the Lord," it became "prove it." Miracles were now considered primitive anomalies, emotional expressions, or cultural myths—relics of a less enlightened time.

Enter thinkers like David Hume, who famously argued that miracles were violations of the laws of nature and, by definition, could never be credible. If something couldn't be repeated under the same conditions, it wasn't considered knowledge. The scientific method, helpful in laboratories, became a spiritual filter—and anything that didn't fit was discarded.[5]

Even within the church, skepticism crept in quietly. Theologians began to separate the "Jesus of history" from the "Christ of faith." The Bible was

---

5. Hume discusses this in section 10 of his *Enquiry Concerning Human Understanding*.

subjected to dissection, not devotion. Seminaries became more concerned with form criticism than faith formation.

In a world powered by logic, mystery became uncomfortable. And many pastors, hoping to stay culturally credible, learned to downplay the miraculous and emphasize the moral. Christianity was recast as an ethical system rather than a supernatural community. Churches became clean, respectable, and largely powerless.

DOCTRINE WITHOUT DEMONSTRATION

A new kind of church emerged: intellectually sharp, socially acceptable, theologically sophisticated . . . and spiritually dry. Creeds were affirmed, but the upper room was abandoned. The stories of Acts were treated like family folklore—fascinating, but not repeatable.

The church still bore the name but had unplugged the power source. It was as if the battery was removed and replaced with a manual: technical, detailed, and completely incapable of making the thing run. They lost the understanding that the car was actually meant to move.

Theologian Jürgen Moltmann captured it clearly: "Without the Holy Spirit there is no living church, only a dead institution. A church without the Spirit is a church without hope."[6] And yet that is precisely what many Western churches had become. Hoping to appear intellectually credible, they forfeited spiritual credibility.

THE COST OF CONTROL

To the Enlightenment-influenced mind, anything unexplainable must be untrue—or at least untrustworthy. And so, the church learned to control what it couldn't confidently explain.

Prayer was domesticated. Preaching was polished. Worship was dignified. And the Spirit? Well, he was acknowledged, but not expected. We didn't deny the Third Person of the Trinity. We just treated him like a silent partner. What resulted was a Christianity that looked impressive on paper but lacked propulsion in real life.

---

6. Moltmann, *Church in the Power*, 64.

And in many places today, the legacy of that shift remains. The church has blueprints and budgets, doctrinal statements and digital campuses. But often, the Spirit is still in the garage: uninvited, unaccessed, and unplugged.

DORMANT ORTHODOXY—SAFE BUT POWERLESS

The impact of Enlightenment rationalism didn't just reshape the eighteenth and nineteenth centuries, it laid the theological and cultural groundwork for what much of the Western church would become in the twentieth: orthodox, organized, and increasingly ornamental.

By the twentieth century, the Western church had settled into a quiet, predictable rhythm, holding fast to creeds and Scriptures but losing the vibrant pulse of Acts. Mainline denominations, once brimming with purpose, saw their vitality fade, attendance dwindled, conversions slowed, and mission drifted toward routine.

From the outside, everything seemed stable: sermons were polished, choirs sang beautifully, buildings stood well kept. Yet, beneath this orderly surface, something essential was missing. The church had become like a finely crafted sailboat, anchored in calm waters, its sails neatly furled, unmoved by the wind of the Spirit.

AN ANEMIC MISSION

When the Spirit's power fades, the church still tries to carry out its mission, but the effort feels empty, lacking divine strength. The Great Commission morphs into committee meetings, evangelism becomes branding, holiness turns into checklists, and justice shrinks to activism without God's authority.

We've built community centers with steeples, offering practical life skills instead of the transformative power of the gospel. Though revival movements, like those led by D. L. Moody, Evan Roberts, Aimee Semple McPherson, Azusa Street, or the Jesus People, briefly rekindled the fire, the institutional church often dismissed them as oddities rather than blueprints for what God intends.

Early Pentecostal tent meetings saw songs interrupted by testimonies, sermons stopped by conviction, even children speaking God's words. These gatherings weren't perfect, but they were alive, pulsing with his presence, not our plans.

Not the Way It's Supposed to Be

A DIFFERENT KIND OF GATHERING

This tame religion stands in sharp contrast to the raw, Spirit-led gatherings of historic awakenings. During the Welsh Revival of 1904–1905, services unfolded without sermons, filled instead with heartfelt worship, fervent prayer, and spontaneous testimonies, the Spirit's presence so overwhelming that worshipers were moved to their knees. At Azusa Street from 1906 to 1909, William Seymour prayed humbly, waiting for God's direction, as healings, prophecies, and tears broke out freely, unbound by any schedule.

WHEN CHURCH BECOMES PREDICTABLE: A SUNDAY WITHOUT SURPRISE

Acts began with waiting: quiet, hungry, expectant. "Wait for the Father's promise.... 'You will be baptized with the Holy Spirit'" (Acts 1:4–5). Heaven answered with fire. But we've traded waiting for schedules, expectancy for routine. Sunday services run like clockwork: a warm welcome, a few practiced songs, an offering, a practical sermon, a tidy closing—all in sixty minutes. It's smooth, polished, predictable. We've planned out every moment, leaving no room for God to surprise us. We've turned church into an event, not an encounter with the living God. And then, it's off to brunch.

THE DANGER OF PREDICTABLE CHRISTIANITY

When church becomes entirely predictable, it becomes entirely manageable. And when we can manage it without God, we will.

We fill the hour with transitions, humor, and production, but too often leave unchanged because we never encountered the God we had come to visit. It's no longer "Not by strength or by might, but by My Spirit" (Zech 4:6)—it's by schedules and sound systems.

....

The church was not called to impress audiences but to ignite disciples. Where power is replaced with polish, the presence of God is ghosted—and the drift accelerates unchecked.

....

Our services flow, but they don't burn. With all our resources, we're losing ground in a world we're called to reach—not because we lack effort, but because we've lost connection. We don't need flashier stages or longer meetings. We need hearts open, surrendered, ready for God to show up.

WHAT HAPPENS WITHOUT THE SPIRIT?

When the church disconnects from the power and presence of the Holy Spirit, we don't simply become less supernatural, we become less Christian. The very essence of New Testament faith is Spirit-born, Spirit-filled, and Spirit-led. Without him, we are a body without breath. A house without heat. A car without a charge.

Churches start explaining away what Scripture makes plain. Miracles are reinterpreted. The gifts of the Spirit are shelved. The book of Acts becomes a museum of what God used to do.

So, what happens when the Spirit is no longer central?

We still have church . . . but something vital is missing.

THEOLOGICAL OUTCOMES: DOCTRINE WITHOUT DYNAMITE

Imagine a fire that once warmed a home, now reduced to embers, barely glowing. That's where we find ourselves in the church today. We cherish our theology, carefully crafted creeds, studied Scriptures, lessons about the Spirit—but something has shifted. Our teaching informs minds but rarely stirs hearts.

The book of Acts, alive with miracles and bold faith, feels like a distant story, a record of what God once did, not what he's doing now. We've leaned into scholarly confidence, parsing Greek verbs and debating doctrines, yet have lost the childlike wonder that expects God to move.

Even entire movements that once carried the fire can drift toward form. The Vineyard, under John Wimber, was once a global voice calling the church back to power evangelism, healing, and intimacy with the Spirit. Wimber famously said, "The Church is so subnormal that if it ever got back to the New Testament normal, it would seem to people to be abnormal."[7]

---

7. Wimber, quoted in Jackson, *Quest for the Radical Middle*, 142.

He taught that "everyone gets to play," not just the professionals. He modeled Spirit-led ministry with accessible theology.

The cry of "Come, Holy Spirit" was gradually replaced—sometimes quietly—with an unspoken caution: "Let's not make people uncomfortable."[8]

When theology is separated from encounter, the church may retain doctrinal integrity but lose its spiritual voltage. The Scriptures are still read. The creeds are still recited. But the dynamite has been defused.

MODERN EVANGELICALISM: INHERITING THE HOLLOW SHELL

As the twentieth century dawned, Evangelicalism rose from the ruins of modernist theology, valiantly defending biblical inerrancy, personal salvation, and the centrality of the cross. But while it guarded the form, it too often surrendered the fire.

And yet, in many ways, it merely inherited the hollowed-out shell of a post-Enlightenment Christianity—"Stockholm Syndrome Christianity"—orthodox in doctrine but anemic in power. Theologically sharp but spiritually numb.

Evangelicalism rightly reacted to liberalism, but in the process, it often unknowingly absorbed the same rationalistic assumptions. It became what might be called functional deism—affirming the Holy Spirit on paper while sidelining him in practice.

In 1970, Christian philosopher Francis Schaeffer addressed the dilemma the church faced regarding its relevance amid a rapidly changing culture that had severed itself from reason. His concern was not that Christianity itself had become irrelevant—he knew that wasn't the case—but rather that the church had lost its bearings. It was no longer producing a revolutionary and authentic Christianity capable of transformation. As a result, Schaeffer believed that the clear majority of Christians lived as practical atheists. Christ might reside in their hearts, but there was little evidence of his presence in their lives.

To illustrate this, Schaeffer proposed a hypothetical:

> Suppose we awoke tomorrow morning and we opened our Bibles and found two things had been taken out—not as the liberals would take them out, but really out. Suppose God had taken them out. The first item missing was the real empowering of the Holy Spirit and

---

8. Jackson, *Quest for the Radical Middle*, 245.

the second item, the reality of prayer. Consequently, following the dictates of Scripture, we would begin to live on the basis of this new Bible in which there was nothing about the Holy Spirit and nothing about the power of prayer. Let me ask you something: What difference would there be from the way we acted yesterday? Do we really believe God is there? If we do, we live differently.[9]

The tragic truth Schaeffer spotlighted—the operation of church life without the Holy Spirit or prayer—is not just conceivable; it's alarmingly common.[10] Schaeffer wasn't only diagnosing the church at the end of the twentieth century, his critique reverberates into the twenty-first. Another Francis, Francis Chan, coauthored a book titled *Forgotten God*,[11] implying that Christians have simply misplaced the Spirit. But in light of Barna's findings, the problem goes far deeper than forgetfulness. It's not a memory lapse—it's a crisis of presence and power.

•••••••••••••••••••••••••••••••••

Caution in the face of God's presence is not wisdom, it is unbelief dressed in respectability. The Spirit will not be managed, and the church will not be revived until his fire is welcomed again.

•••••••••••••••••••••••••••••••••

That sentiment echoes the tragic moment in Samson's life: "He did not know that the LORD had left him" (Judg 16:20).

Evangelicalism has excelled at preaching, publishing, and programming. But too often, it has neglected presence. Services are timed. Sermons are branded. Leadership is borrowed from the marketplace. We have learned how to grow churches without God.

It's the equivalent of owning a state-of-the-art Tesla: beautiful, intelligent, loaded with features... and then keeping it unplugged in the garage. We still sit in it. We still polish it. But we don't go anywhere because we've forgotten to connect it to power. And, perhaps worse than that, we've forgotten it actually needs power.

9. Schaeffer, *Church at the End*, 47.
10. Barna Group, "Most American Christians."
11. Chan and Yankoski, *Forgotten God*.

Even revival movements have not been immune. The Jesus Movement. The seeker-sensitive wave. The megachurch boom. All emphasized relevance and renewal, but many stopped short of full reengagement with the New Testament charisms. The Spirit is welcomed in word but restrained in practice.

Dallas Willard observed, "The greatest issue facing the world today... is whether those who are identified as 'Christians' will become disciples—students, apprentices, practitioners—of Jesus Christ, steadily learning from Him how to live the life of the Kingdom of Heaven into every corner of human existence."[12]

Yet without the empowering of the Spirit, such discipleship becomes moralism dressed in religious language. J. P. Moreland lamented, "We have lost our grasp on the reality of the unseen world and the power of the Spirit.... The church has become a shell of its potential because it no longer expects God to actually act."[13]

These aren't fringe critiques. They are a mirror held up to much of the contemporary church: doctrinally sound, spiritually starved. A faith that intellectually affirms Pentecost while practically ignoring it. A movement that began in fire and now runs on fumes.

To inherit the hollow shell means to maintain the form of godliness while denying its power (2 Tim 3:5). It means singing about the Spirit while systemically avoiding any true encounter. It means building services and strategies around human ingenuity rather than divine leading.

It is the logical conclusion of centuries of slow, subtle abandonment, not of theology but of life in the Spirit. And yet, even in this hollow state, the ember remains. God is not finished with his church. But he waits for the church to recognize what it has lost—and repent.

THE CHURCH THAT FORGOT IT WAS CAPTIVE

If the problem were merely powerlessness, we could seek renewal. The deeper tragedy is that it no longer notices, or cares. We've grown comfortable without it!

Like prisoners who have grown fond of their captors, we have acclimated to our captivity. The fire is gone, but we call the ashes maturity. The gifts are missing, but we call it balance. The voice of the Spirit is silent, but

---

12. Willard, *Great Omission*, 11.
13. Moreland, *Kingdom Triangle*, 157.

we defend our silence as prudence. This is not just drift. This is delusion. This is Stockholm Syndrome Christianity.

We have adopted the powerlessness of the very culture we were called to confront. The church, meant to be a Spirit-filled resistance movement, has become a state-sanctioned chaplaincy to the culture of unbelief. It imitates what it should indict. It accommodates what it should transform. And it denies the power it desperately needs, because to acknowledge that loss would require painful repentance. The result is paralysis.

Our liturgies may be ancient and our theology may be orthodox, but our ministry is often lifeless. We host conferences on church growth while ignoring the fact that we are no longer dangerous to the gates of hell. We have been subdued not by persecution but by co-optation. Like the Israelites in exile, many have forgotten who they are and where they belong. We preach about the resurrection but live as though Pentecost never happened. We defend the Bible but rarely demonstrate its power. We lift our hands in worship but keep our hearts closed to the Spirit. We say we believe in miracles but build systems that ensure we'll never need one.

We have inherited a faith once marked by fire and reduced it to a flicker. We are not just lukewarm. We are spiritually ghosted. And the silence is deafening.

Even now, in our seminaries and pulpits, the pattern persists. Future pastors are trained to explain the faith but not embody its power. We teach apologetics without authority, theology without intimacy, homiletics without holiness. The church continues to perpetuate the great forgetting, handing down a version of Christianity that is rational, respectable, ... and radically disempowered.

We are being ghosted. Not by the Spirit, but by our own refusal to welcome him.

And so we ask, What does it mean to follow Jesus in the absence of power? What happens when the Spirit is absent, not by divine judgment but by design?

The church's slow drift into spiritual vacancy has not occurred in a vacuum. It has been curated, defended, and perpetuated—often by well-meaning leaders who have learned to function in the absence of fire. While pews grow quiet, pulpits grow polished. And the silence of the Spirit is matched only by the silence of the shepherds.

If we are being ghosted, it is not simply because the Spirit has withdrawn—it is because we have trained a generation of leaders not to miss him when he's gone.

CHAPTER 3

Ghosted: Silence of the Shepherds

> The simple step of a courageous individual is not to take part in the lie.
> One word of truth outweighs the world.
>
> —ALEKSANDR SOLZHENITSYN, *GULAG ARCHIPELAGO*

IN OUR CULTURAL LEXICON, "ghosting" typically refers to someone who suddenly cuts off all communication—no explanation, no closure, just silence. It's a relational vanishing act. And while it often occurs in dating or friendships, the term has never been more tragically appropriate for the modern church.

Ghosting has two distinct, but inseparable, meanings for us. The church has ghosted the Spirit, and it has ghosted its witness. One is vertical; the other, horizontal. But they are two sides of the same spiritual collapse.

To ghost the Spirit is to quietly back away from the power and presence of God. It is to preach about Pentecost without expecting power, to sing about the Holy Spirit while avoiding the gifts, and to substitute fog machines for fire. The Spirit is still speaking, but many pulpits are no longer listening.

To ghost our witness is to withdraw from our prophetic role in the world. It is to grow silent when the culture needs clarity. It is to choose peace over truth, popularity over obedience, and programming over proclamation. Silence, in this context, is not neutral. It is capitulation. Silence is ghosting. Not speaking is speaking. Not standing is bowing.

Ghosted: Silence of the Shepherds

This chapter marks the final movement in section 1: "Crisis of Capitulation." If the church is to reclaim her voice, it must begin by admitting she's lost it. We cannot restore what we refuse to acknowledge is broken. We cannot crash the gates if we're still cowering in front of them.

Let us then consider what happens when the shepherds, those entrusted with the mouthpiece of heaven, go quiet.

A DEAFENING SILENCE

The most dangerous silence is not the one imposed from the outside—but the one embraced on the inside. The modern church, and particularly its leaders, have not simply been silenced by external forces, they have ghosted the Spirit and muted the voice of God from within. In a time when boldness is demanded, we whisper. In a world starved for truth, we self-censor. In an age of chaos, the church has lost her sound.

This is not merely a corporate issue, it is deeply personal. The silence is systemic, yes, but its roots are individual, spiritual, and moral. Stockholm Syndrome Christianity is what happens when the church starts siding with her captors instead of her calling. We have become comfortable in our captivity. The cultural kidnappers offer social credibility, institutional safety, and algorithmic applause—and in exchange, we muzzle our message. Like prisoners who've fallen in love with their warden, we have confused peace with paralysis.

> *Every generation has a choice: speak with clarity or vanish into compromise. Silence may feel safe, but it always leaves the flock exposed and the culture unconfronted.*

The result? A church that blends in rather than stands out. Leaders who shrink back instead of step forward. A body that is functionally mute in the marketplace of ideas, terrified of offending and addicted to being liked. This isn't what Jesus envisioned when he said, "You are the light of the world. A city set on a hill cannot be hidden" (Matt 5:14). But that light has dimmed. And it didn't happen overnight. It happened because we stopped speaking. We stopped warning. We stopped proclaiming.

When the Holy Spirit was ghosted, the prophetic voice of the church went with him. The Spirit doesn't just comfort—he convicts. He doesn't merely guide—he galvanizes. And where he is not welcomed, silence fills the vacuum. Pastors stopped preaching with power because they stopped praying with passion. They became sidetracked with planning and preparing for next week's Sunday episode.

Congregations stopped engaging with courage because they stopped encountering the presence. The Holy Spirit was demoted from the engine to the echo; mentioned in creeds, but absent in character and courage.

As Francis Schaeffer reminded us in the last chapter, the brutal truth is that in far too many churches, the Spirit's absence changes nothing. Our services continue. Our plans unfold. Our metrics might even improve. But our power would be fake, our influence hollow, and our gospel muted.

We are not here just to manage religious services, we are here to proclaim kingdom realities. But proclamation requires presence. And presence requires power. And power requires the Holy Spirit. When we ghost him, we lose the source of our voice.

This silence is not benign. It is disobedience dressed as diplomacy. It is cowardice cloaked in cultural relevance. And worst of all, it is contagious. Ghosted leaders raise ghosted congregants. Silence in the pulpit leads to apathy in the pews.

It is not enough to blame the culture. The real indictment is that the church has gone quiet, not because she was gagged but because she consented. This silence was already growing before any external crisis hit. But in 2020, a global pandemic would strip away every excuse and reveal just how deep our capitulation had gone.

COVID-19 AND THE COLLAPSE OF COURAGE

The global pandemic did not cause the collapse of courage in the church, but it did reveal it. COVID became a stress test that exposed the spiritual brittleness of much of Western Christianity. What we learned in those months of crisis was that many pastors, pulpits, and parishioners were far more conditioned by fear than formed by faith.

Churches closed not just their buildings but their mouths. Many of the very leaders called to shepherd their flocks through the valley of the shadow of death chose instead to echo talking points, bow to pressure, and

Ghosted: Silence of the Shepherds

outsource their leadership to secular authorities. In doing so, they didn't just submit to health protocols, they abdicated prophetic responsibility.

According to Barna, 69 percent of pastors report feeling pressure from within their own congregations when addressing political or social issues.[1] This pressure didn't just shape tone—it shaped content. Sermons were filtered through the lens of public approval rather than biblical authority. The pulpit became a tightrope walk of cultural diplomacy. And while the world faced mortality, the church forfeited its moment.

For the first time in a generation, our culture was forced to confront death, uncertainty, and human limitation: prime soil for gospel proclamation. And instead of seizing the hour, many churches sanitized their message, shifted to online production, and quietly complied with ever-changing rules. In doing so, we failed to offer what no one else could: supernatural hope in the face of mortal fear.

The result was not neutral—it was spiritually devastating. Instead of being known for boldness, the church became known for silence or compromise.

National data confirms the severity of this spiritual retreat. In March 2020, 99 percent of pastors reported suspending in-person worship, and by April, 93 percent had pivoted to online-only services.[2] Churches were no longer gathering in community, they were retreating into pixels and passivity.

Instead of being the voice of courage, we were often the echo of culture. We became, as Os Guinness warned in *A Free People's Suicide*, "a people who valued freedom, but not the virtue required to sustain it."[3]

COVID didn't invent Stockholm Christianity, it simply unmasked and accelerated it. It was the perfect storm to expose a long-standing weakness: we had become institutional caretakers rather than Spirit-empowered heralds. The very pastors who should have stood in the gap for their cities instead retreated into virtual platforms and political neutrality.

When the government declared certain businesses and gatherings essential but labeled the church nonessential, where were the shepherds?

Some, to be sure, stood strong. They continued gathering, praying, and proclaiming. But many more did not. They feared fines more than forsaking the assembly. They feared reputational loss more than spiritual impotence.

1. Barna Group, "Pastors Face Communication Challenges."
2. McConnell, "Pastors, Churches."
3. Guinness, *Free People's Suicide*, 23.

And their silence discipled their congregations more than their sermons did. The pattern was consistent: when external pressures mounted, internal confidence withered. Barna Research found that only 34 percent of pastors felt comfortable publicly challenging government mandates, even when they believed churches were being unfairly restricted.[4] This reluctance was not merely pragmatic, it was spiritual. And it revealed just how ghosted the prophetic role of the pastor had become.

This is not to suggest recklessness or rebellion for its own sake. But when the Spirit is ghosted in favor of government approval, we must ask, Whom do we really serve? Whose voice do we obey? And whose example are we following? Because the church that walks the path of Jonah during a crisis will never speak like Jesus in revival.

And the fallout was staggering. Barna reports that one in three practicing Christians stopped attending church altogether, online or in-person, during the pandemic.[5] Ghosted by their leaders and disconnected from community, many never returned.

It is time to confront the brutal truth: the collapse of courage during COVID was not a fluke. It was the predictable result of decades of spiritual drift. And unless we learn from it, we will repeat it—next time with even greater consequences.

The call of the Stockdale Church is not denial. It is resolve. It is seeing the failure of the past season and deciding it will not define the next one.

We have ghosted the Spirit long enough. It is time to repent, stand, and speak. The pandemic revealed not only a collapse of courage but also how easily the church will outsource her voice to the state when pressured. COVID tested our resolve; now we must examine how law and policy have deepened the chill and why so many pulpits went quiet even without legal force.

WHEN GOVERNMENT MUZZLES THE PULPIT

In a nation founded on the freedom of religion and the freedom of speech, it is a dark irony that many pastors have voluntarily silenced themselves. But this is no new battle. In 1954, then Senator Lyndon B. Johnson inserted an amendment into the federal tax code—now infamously known as the

---

4. Stone, "US Pastors Grappling."
5. Barna Group, "Signs of Decline and Hope."

Johnson Amendment—which prohibited 501(c)(3) tax-exempt organizations, including churches, from endorsing or opposing political candidates.

What was originally intended as a retaliatory political maneuver has become one of the most effective muzzling tools against the American church. While it has rarely been enforced with legal action, its chilling effect has been profound. Thousands of pastors, fearing the loss of tax-exempt status or simply the scrutiny of government oversight, have chosen silence over boldness. The amendment, though small in scope, successfully created a culture of caution.

But legal caution has metastasized into theological capitulation. We no longer merely avoid political endorsements—we avoid moral clarity. Many pastors who once thundered truth now tiptoe through nuance. They preach sanitized messages that keep the peace but lose the power. As a result, the prophetic voice of the pulpit has been neutered, not by the government directly but by the internal compromise of leaders unwilling to risk offense.

The US Constitution enshrines the free exercise of religion. The pulpits of America are not subject to IRS approval, but they've been behaving as if they were. This is not simply about politics. It is about prophetic responsibility. The Bible is filled with men and women who spoke truth to power. Moses confronted Pharaoh. Nathan confronted David. Elijah confronted Ahab. John the Baptist confronted Herod. Paul confronted Caesar's courts. None of them worried about the tax code.

The real tragedy is not that the government tried to quiet the church, it's that the church agreed. We have ghosted our prophetic responsibility and, in doing so, handed over cultural ground we were commissioned to occupy. We've abandoned the gates of influence: media, politics, education, law . . . and in our absence, darkness has filled the void.

But perhaps even more dangerous than external censorship is internal cowardice. The government may muzzle from the outside, but when the church muzzles itself, the damage spreads exponentially. It becomes systemic, self-sustaining, and spiritually terminal.

I remember standing in the pulpit of a Southern California church where I served as a teaching pastor for twelve years. The senior pastor was away, and I was scheduled to speak during the heart of the COVID pandemic—just weeks before the 2020 election. I urged the congregation to reject fear, to reclaim their voice, and to speak boldly as mouthpieces of God in a cultural moment of chaos.

Days before the message, I had asked the senior pastor if I could address the political tension in my closing comments. He gave me permission. So I spoke plainly. I urged our people to vote biblically, explaining the moral contrasts between the political platforms—not personalities—and reminding them we weren't electing a pastor but a president.

After the service, a prominent member approached me. He was outraged. He had texted the senior pastor mid-sermon to ask if he knew what I was saying. The pastor replied to him, "I never gave him permission to do that."

In that moment, it became crystal clear: the issue wasn't just what the government might do to the church. It was what the church was already doing to itself.

They were content to operate within their four walls, perfectly satisfied with programs and potlucks, so long as no one dared challenge the idols outside. It was not government mandates that silenced them—it was spiritual myopia and fear.

Stockholm Christianity hides behind the Johnson Amendment as a convenient excuse. But the Stockdale Church sees through the fog. It knows that true courage is not the same as picking sides in politics, and it recognizes that staying silent is never neutral—it is surrender.

This is not about endorsing parties. It's about proclaiming principles. It's about declaring that righteousness still exalts a nation (Prov 14:34), that injustice must be named, and that sin must be confronted, no matter who holds office.

The pulpits of old once echoed with fire. Today, many echo with fluff. But the silence must be broken. Not recklessly. Not arrogantly. But boldly, lovingly, and fearlessly.

Because the government does not determine the boundaries of God's call. Caesar may claim jurisdiction, but Christ commands obedience. And he still calls his prophets to speak truth, even when the state frowns upon it.

Now is the time for the shepherds to rise. To reclaim their voice. To realize that they do not serve a party—they serve a King. If we do not speak, who will? If we do not stand, who can? If the pulpits remain ghosted, the people will remain lost.

The truth is, the government can muzzle a pulpit from the outside, but only the prophet can choose to stay silent on the inside. Laws may intimidate, but they cannot produce the bitterness, fear, or reluctance that keeps a message locked in the messenger. For that, we need to look not at the state but at the heart. Jonah's heart.

BECOMING JONAH

The story of Jonah is not a fable about a fish; it is a mirror held up to the heart of every reluctant messenger of God. Strip away the Sunday school familiarity and you find a prophet who ghosted his calling, silenced his voice, and resented the very mercy he was sent to proclaim. Jonah is not merely a man who ran from God—he is a prophet who refused to speak. He is the anti-mouthpiece of heaven.

The word of the Lord came to Jonah: "Get up! Go to the great city of Nineveh and preach against it, because their wickedness has confronted Me" (Jon 1:2). It was not a gentle suggestion. It was a divine summons. Jonah was not called to build consensus, strategize outreach, or host a forum. He was called to proclaim. God's command was crystal clear—and Jonah fled.

Why? Because Jonah's problem wasn't uncertainty. It was contempt. He knew exactly what God wanted, and he wanted no part of it. He ghosted his assignment, boarded a ship, and sank into a willful slumber while a storm brewed. The man called to speak went mute. The prophet became a passenger. The mouthpiece became a runaway.

When awakened by pagan sailors, Jonah offered no prayer, no sermon, no prophetic word, just resignation: "Throw me overboard." He would rather drown than obey. He would rather perish than prophesy. Even the fish that swallowed him was more obedient than the prophet inside it.

And when Jonah finally did go to Nineveh, he delivered the bare minimum: an eight-word sermon. No compassion. No invitation. No warning. Just judgment. And when the city repented, when the people humbled themselves in sackcloth and ashes, Jonah became angry. "I know that You are a merciful and compassionate God," he complained (Jon 4:2). He resented their redemption. He sulked in the shade, hoping for wrath.

THIS IS NOT JUST JONAH'S STORY—IT IS OURS

Consider Judson Cornwall, a prolific charismatic preacher who once harbored deep-seated resentment toward Germans due to wartime memories. When invited to speak at a revival in Germany, he contemptuously threw away the invitation. But it haunted him until, prodded by his wife, he retrieved it and surrendered to the call.

As he arrived at the conference, held in the former SS headquarters, old prejudices resurfaced. He prayed, fasted, and avoided the attendees until, in a moment of spiritual confrontation, God revealed, "You have no authority here because you do not love these people."[6]

Overwhelmed, Cornwall repented. The next morning, he greeted the attendees with genuine affection, even embracing his translator, and preached under the weight of God's love, not guilt. Many responded by forgiving past wounds, testifying to the healing that only love through obedience can effect.[7]

The parallels are striking. We, too, have received a word from the Lord. We, too, are surrounded by cities under judgment. Yet, like Jonah and Cornwall, we board ships of distraction, slumber through storms, and speak from a safe distance. We've whispered instead of warning, posted instead of preaching, wavered instead of weeping.

Some pastors mirror this same posture—anchored in correctness but estranged from compassion. They preach against Nineveh rather than walk its streets or sit at its tables.

This is why Jonah must be retrieved, not as Sunday school nostalgia but as a prophetic warning to the "Stockholm Christian" who isolates in fear, preaching without mercy.

We are Jonah. And, unless we repent, we will remain trapped in silence.

But there is another way. The Stockdale Church faces the hard assignments, sees its captivity, owns its compromise, and reclaims the voice it once ghosted. It hears, "Cry out! Proclaim! Speak my word!" (see Jon 3:1–2), and it does not run because the Spirit is still speaking. But he will not speak through a silenced church. The call is personal. It is corporate. And it is now.

Jonah's story ends not in resolution but with God's piercing question: "Should I not care about the great city of Nineveh?" (Jon 4:11). That question still echoes: Should God not be concerned about this generation, this city, this nation? And if so, why are his messengers asleep?

Let us not end our story like Jonah: disconnected, resentful, unwilling. Let us rise, gripped by the Spirit, awakened to our call, and ready to speak

---

6. Ponsonby, *Loving Mercy*, 23–24.
7. Ponsonby, *Loving Mercy*, 22–24.

again. Because when the messenger's heart goes silent, the message itself goes missing.

WHEN THE MOUTH GOES QUIET... THE CHURCH GOES COLD

When the voice of the church is absent, her heart withers—and when the heart goes cold, the culture soon follows. Silence from the sanctuary leads to decay in the streets. This is not a theoretical concern, it is a documented biblical reality.

In Hos 4:1–3, the word of the Lord comes as an indictment not against the pagans, but against the priests:

> Hear the word of the LORD, people of Israel,
> for the LORD has a case
> against the inhabitants of the land:
> There is no truth, no faithful love,
> and no knowledge of God in the land!
> Cursing, lying, murder, stealing,
> and adultery are rampant;
> one act of bloodshed follows another.
> For this reason the land mourns,
> and everyone who lives in it languishes,
> along with the wild animals and the birds of the sky;
> even the fish of the sea disappear.

But the word of the Lord is not to the pagan culture, it is to the priests. The mouthpieces of God. Verse 6 confirms this when Hosea writes,

> My people are destroyed for lack of knowledge.
> Because you have rejected knowledge,
> I will reject you from serving as My priest.
> Since you have forgotten the law of your God,
> I will also forget your sons.

This rebuke lands squarely on the shoulders of the spiritual leaders who had failed to steward the knowledge of God into the cultural bloodstream. The failure was not that the culture was corrupt—it was that the priests were silent.

This same prophetic charge echoes in our day. Where is the truth? Where is the faithful love? Where is the knowledge of God in our public discourse, our school systems, our legislatures, our media? When the church refuses to confront sin, corruption, and idolatry with the truth and presence of God, it forfeits its role as salt and light. The watchmen on the walls have grown silent—and as Ezek 33 warns, their blood will be on our hands.

We are not the first generation to face this crisis. But history reveals that those who made a difference were those who refused to stay silent. Dietrich Bonhoeffer stood against the Nazi regime and the capitulating German church, declaring, "Silence in the face of evil is itself evil."[8] He did not wait for cultural permission. He acted prophetically in a time of cowardice and compromise—and ultimately paid with his life.

Charles Finney, a revivalist and theologian, did not separate evangelism from activism. He thundered against the sin of slavery and called the church to repentance, saying, "The church must take right ground in regard to politics. . . . The time has come that Christians must vote for honest men and take consistent ground in politics."[9] Finney did not see preaching as separate from cultural confrontation; he saw them as inseparable.

William Wilberforce, driven by Christian conviction, spent his life fighting the slave trade in Britain. He saw the gospel as not only a personal reality but a public responsibility. His tireless advocacy led to the abolition of slavery—proof that one man, gripped by the Spirit, can reshape a nation.[10]

These were not extremists. They were reformers. They understood that a gospel which does not touch culture has not touched the church. They opened their mouths and moved their feet.

Contrast that with today's pulpits, where sermons are polished but powerless and church programs are sophisticated but spiritually sterile. When our preaching stays inside the walls, we cease to fulfill the Great Commission. When our witness is limited to Sunday services, we have traded apostleship for audience-building.

We are not called to manage the decline; we are called to spark reformation. And reformation begins when we recover our voice. Not merely to speak louder, but to speak rightly, boldly, and prophetically into every sphere of influence.

Our culture is not just lost—it is sick, cancerous, and in full rebellion against the knowledge of God. But the answer is not better branding. It is a

---

8. Metaxas, *Bonhoeffer*, 281.
9. Finney, *Lectures on Revivals*, 281.
10. Metaxas, *Amazing Grace*.

bold, Spirit-filled church that dares to speak again. Because the church that speaks only to herself has ceased to be the church.

The Great Commission was never meant to be fulfilled in a holy huddle. It is a call to preach to the nations, to confront kings and courts, to disciple cities and nations. And if we are to be the reformers of our generation, we must reject the silence of Stockholm and embrace the courage of Stockdale.

Our mouths must open. Our hands must move. Our hearts must burn.

WHAT WE LOST ... AND CAN STILL REGAIN

The ghosting of the Spirit has cost us far more than emotional fervor—it has stripped the church of her vitality, clarity, and authority. What we've lost is not merely stylistic or generational. We've lost our edge. We've lost our supernatural witness. We've lost the very power that distinguished the church from every other institution on earth.

At the heart of this loss is a forfeited dependency. The early church did not merely talk about God, they walked in the authority and anointing of the Spirit. Miracles, prophetic words, bold preaching, supernatural discernment—these were not rare exceptions but normative expressions of a Spirit-empowered community. When Peter stood on Pentecost, he did not stand alone; he stood filled. When Paul confronted Elymas,[11] it wasn't charisma; it was power. When Stephen faced death, his face shone with heaven's glory, and his lips overflowed with forgiveness.

These weren't anomalies—they were archetypes. They modeled what happens when the Spirit of God is not just a doctrine, but a Person present and active. That presence is what we've lost. And without him, our services may look successful, but they will lack spiritual substance. We may grow in number, but shrink in power.

Rodney Stark, in his sociological study, *The Rise of Christianity*, documents how the early church exploded in influence, not through comfort or compromise but through costly love.

> The impact of Christian mercy was dramatic. In the midst of the second-century Antonine plague and the third-century Cyprian plague, while pagans fled, Christians stayed. They cared for the sick, buried the dead, and risked their lives for others. . . . This care and courage made Christianity attractive—its doctrine was validated by

11. Acts 13:8–10.

action. . . . Their doctrine provided a prescription for action. . . . Mercy and self-sacrifice became their apologetic.[12]

In contrast, our generation fled the public square. We sanitized our sermons, outsourced our courage, and traded eternal influence for digital applause.

What was ghosted? Our witness. And our witness was always meant to be more than words. It was meant to be word and power. Salt and light. Gospel and fire.

But here is the hope: it can be regained. The gifts of the Spirit were never revoked. I dare you to find a single passage that says so. The call to courage never rescinded. The invitation to boldness never retracted. The Spirit still groans, still calls, still empowers. But he will not fill what is content to stay empty. He will not empower what refuses to engage. He will not revive what refuses to repent.

We must acknowledge what's missing. We must grieve what we forfeited. And we must hunger again, not for relevance but for righteousness. Not for applause but for anointing. Not for popularity but for presence.

The Stockdale Church confronts what it has lost without losing hope. It names the vacuum and invites the Spirit back in to fill it. The Stockholm Church makes peace with decline. The Stockdale Church prepares for Pentecost.

Everything we lost, we can still regain if we humble ourselves, seek his face, and open wide the doors we once shut.

FROM GHOSTED TO GRIPPED

We now arrive at a threshold moment, not only the conclusion of this chapter but the conclusion of section 1: "Crisis of Capitulation." This has not been a theoretical analysis of the church's decline; it has been an unmasking. We have not simply traced historical failure; we've stared into a mirror. It's not just them—it's us.

We have ghosted the Spirit. We have silenced our witness. We have retreated from the gates we were commissioned to crash. But as with Jonah, the word of the Lord comes to us a second time (Jon 3:1). God still calls. God still empowers. God still sends. And his invitation remains open—not for preservation, but transformation.

---

12. Stark, *Rise of Christianity*, 82–83.

Ghosted: Silence of the Shepherds

This is the turn. The hinge. The moment where Stockholm surrender is cast aside and Stockdale courage takes root. The indictment has been delivered, but so has the opportunity. The gates of hell still tremble—not at our branding, but at our boldness. Not at our numbers, but at our anointing. Not at our polish, but at our power.

To be gripped by the Spirit is to take your place in the collision of heaven and earth. It is to rise like Elijah, speak like Peter, and weep like Jeremiah. It is to burn, not with rage but with righteousness. It is to go where Jonah fled. To speak where Jonah sulked. To love where Jonah judged. To reclaim the prophetic voice the church was born to carry.

To be gripped is to be revived, recalibrated, and recommissioned. It is to remember that the Holy Spirit is not a concept to be debated but a Person to be followed into the fire, into the culture, into the courts of kings and the alleys of the forgotten. It is to find your spine in his strength, your voice in his wind, your tears in his burden.

We have grown comfortable ghosting the Spirit because we feared what he might ask of us. But to be gripped means that we no longer fear obedience more than obscurity. We long no longer for ease but for effect—for the sound of gates breaking and captives being set free.

Every reformation began with someone who let the Spirit grip them beyond convenience and beyond control. Martin Luther nailed his *Ninety-Five Theses* because he was gripped. John Wesley rode on horseback from church to church because he was gripped. Corrie ten Boom hid the persecuted because she was gripped. These were ordinary saints made extraordinary by surrender. We are not at the end. We are at the edge.

WATCHMEN OR WALLFLOWERS?

The watchman is not optional. In biblical imagery, the watchman stood atop the city walls, scanning the horizon for threats and calling out with clarity and urgency when danger approached. His failure to sound the alarm was not merely dereliction of duty; it was blood on his hands (Ezek 33).

Today, the role of watchman has been given to the church. But instead of standing guard, many have opted for safety behind stained glass, distracted by strategy meetings and sermon series while the culture burns outside. We have confused niceness with holiness, silence with civility, and passivity with peace.

We weren't called to be wallflowers in Babylon—we were called to be watchmen.

Our failure to warn, confront, and disciple has real-world consequences. Generations are growing up biblically illiterate, morally confused, and spiritually aimless. We've produced attendees, not ambassadors. Fans, not followers. The prophetic has been replaced by the pragmatic, and the result is a church afraid of its own shadow.

A shepherd without a trumpet is a watchman without a wall—and both invite destruction.

And yet, the call remains. As long as Babylon stands, the watchman must speak.

This is not about angry rants or political dog whistles. It's about truth in love. It's about naming sin with compassion and offering grace without dilution. It's about living so rooted in Christ that we cannot help but echo his voice in a world filled with noise.

To be a watchman is to live alert. It is to be like the sons of Issachar and read the times and ready the people. It is to resist the slow erosion of conviction and the pressure to be liked.

And yes, it will cost you. That is the very essence of picking up your cross. It will cost your comfort. It may cost your popularity. In some places, it will cost your freedom.

But it's worth it. Because the wallflower may be safe, but the watchman is faithful. And in the end, it is not the applause of Babylon we seek. It is the commendation of the King: "Well done, good and faithful slave."

THE CHOICE

This chapter, and this first section, ends with a choice. Will we allow this diagnosis to become transformation? Will we respond to the word of the Lord with repentance and resolve? Or . . . will we continue to ghost the Spirit and resume with our programs and sermons to the choir?

The church has always been at its strongest when it stands apart—not above, but distinct—when it names sin, calls for righteousness, and offers hope through repentance. When it speaks truth to power and stands in the gap for the vulnerable.

Today, we must ask, Who silenced us?

And perhaps more urgently, Why did we agree?

The gospel is not politically neutral. It confronts every idol, every ideology, every empire. The gospel is not safe—it's subversive. It dethrones kings, overturns tables, and exposes false shepherds. Os Guinness captures this moment with prophetic precision:

> The Roman republic fell and later the Roman Empire, but there is no need for America to follow. The watching world stands by to witness what you choose and to see whether your illustrious ancestors will find heirs worthy of their vision. Americans, you are America now just as the Athenians were Athens and the Romans were Rome. So the choice is yours—and so too will be the consequences. Let your choice be known, and let it be followed through with courage and resolve. Your hour has struck. Your challenge lies before you, and God and the world and history await your answer.[13]

Guinness concludes each chapter with a sobering warning: "All who aspire to be like Rome in their beginnings must avoid being Rome at their ending."

America is not falling because sinners sin. That's what sinners do. America is faltering because saints are silent. If the church will not stand in Babylon, who will? And if not now, when?

So rise, watchman.

Sound the alarm.

The city is still worth defending.

The King is still on the throne.

Now is the time for resolve—not retreat. Now is the hour to stand—not shrink. Now is the moment to rise—not roll over.

Babylon is watching.

Let them see a church on fire with truth, forged in grace, immovable in love.

Not because we seek confrontation, but because we've been commissioned.

The silence ends here. The gates begin to rattle. The hour for passive Christianity has passed. From this moment forward, the question is not whether we see the crisis; it's whether we are willing to be the cure.

---

13. Guinness, *Free People's Suicide*, 205.

Section 1 has exposed the capitulation. Section 2 will lay the foundation for the fight.

Here we move from diagnosis to design, from naming the problem to building the people who will stand against it.

SECTION TWO

Kingdom Triangle Algorithm

We have named the crisis. Now we take up the cure. The "Kingdom Triangle Algorithm" is not a program or a quick-fix formula; it is heaven's blueprint for a church that refuses to bow and disciples who refuse to break. It is both a theological vision and a practical framework for Spirit-empowered living.

At its heart are three integrated dimensions: life in the Spirit, a renewed mind, and a resilient soul. Each is essential. Each fuels the other. Together, they form the kind of disciple and the kind of church that can crash the gates of hell and stand unshaken in a collapsing culture.

And like any true triangle, one point rises above the rest—the apex. In the Kingdom Triangle, that apex is life in the Spirit. Without him, the other dimensions lose their shape and their strength. With him, they are energized, sharpened, and unstoppable.

In *Kingdom Triangle*, J. P. Moreland outlines three essential dimensions for personal and cultural transformation: the recovery of the Christian mind, the renovation of the soul, and the restoration of the Spirit's power.[1] His order is deliberate. It is crafted to address the intellectual and moral credibility of the faith in a postmodern age. And woven throughout his vision is the conviction that the Spirit's presence is the empowering force for the entire triangle.

In this moment of deep cultural capitulation and spiritual anemia, we must give fresh and urgent attention to what I call the "Spirit Apex."

---

1. Moreland, *Kingdom Triangle*.

The church's greatest need is not merely sharper reasoning or better self-understanding, but a renewed baptism of power from on high. Pentecost was not an afterthought—it was the launch sequence. Jesus' final command wasn't "Go reason together," but "Stay in the city until you are empowered from on high" (Luke 24:49).

We still value the recovery of the mind and the renovation of the soul, but in this present hour we must begin in the "upper room." From that sacred vertex of power, the Spirit energizes both thought and life, igniting the mind with truth and shaping the soul with holiness. Without the apex of the Spirit, the other points of the triangle lose their force. With him, they become unstoppable.

This section, "Kingdom Triangle Algorithm," builds on Moreland's framework, reanchoring the three points with a fresh Spirit-first urgency for our time. It also introduces a fourth chapter, "Power Protocol," as the connective tissue that turns the triangle from a static diagram into a living, breathing algorithm for revival and transformation. Here, the Spirit Apex fuels the mind with truth, the soul with wholeness, and the church with unstoppable force.

Chapter 4 begins our triangle journey: "Spirit Apex." It is here we enter the whirlwind of the Holy Spirit's empowering presence. The church must rediscover the baptism of fire, not as an abstract doctrine but as the catalytic center of New Testament Christianity. This is the upper room in action. Without the Spirit's dynamic, we are simply rearranging furniture in a burning house. With him, the church becomes a force that hell cannot ignore.

In chapter 5, "Christians Have Lost Their Minds!," we reclaim the life of the mind, not as a sterile intellectual exercise but as a Spirit-illuminated faculty designed to engage truth, beauty, and moral clarity. A reformed mind is not enough; it must be renewed by the Spirit and yielded to Christ's lordship so that our thinking is as Spirit-powered as our preaching.

Then in chapter 6, "Shalom Soul vs. the Empty Self," we observe the sharp contrast between two ways of living. One is the fragmented, do-it-yourself identity the world assembles— fragile under the weight of cultural narcissism. The other is the Spirit-renovated soul, completed by God's presence and flourishing in his peace. Here we confront the epidemic of the "empty self" and set it beside the biblical vision of a "Shalom Soul"—a life marked by surrender, integrity, and Spirit-shaped wholeness. True soul

Section Two: Kingdom Triangle Algorithm

health cannot be manufactured through self-help techniques; it flows only from the apex of the Spirit.

Finally, in chapter 7, "Power Protocol," we move from theory to practice. This is where the Kingdom Triangle comes alive in motion. "Power Protocol" is the bridge between encounter and endurance, fire and formation. Here, Spirit, mind, and soul sync into a cohesive, power-infused rhythm for daily life. Without this divine protocol, the triangle remains theory. With it, we become a united, Spirit-charged force, aligned to crash the gates of hell together.

This recalibration is not merely theological—it is strategic. We are preparing to crash the gates of hell. And to do so, we must be fully aligned: empowered by the Spirit, sharpened in mental resolve, grounded in soul-deep peace, and activated by divine protocol. This is not principle on a page—it is a summons to the front lines.

The Kingdom Triangle is not a diagram to admire; it is a battle formation to enter. And once you step into it, you will not come out the same.

Welcome to the triangle.

CHAPTER 4

Spirit Apex

The Spirit as an experienced and living reality was the absolutely crucial matter for Christian life, from beginning to end.

—GORDON FEE, *GOD'S EMPOWERING PRESENCE*

IT DIDN'T HAPPEN IN his seminary classroom. It happened in the dusty heat of Nigeria, where theology collided with power, and Charles Kraft's worldview cracked wide open.

A professor at Fuller Theological Seminary, Kraft had long been shaped by Western theological assumptions: that God worked primarily through natural means, that the miraculous was rare and irregular, and that the spiritual realm operated politely, at a distance. Kraft and his wife went to Nigeria after completing their seminary training. They believed they were well-prepared with linguistic tools and cultural research. Yet, once they arrived, they quickly realized how ill-equipped they were to deal with one of the most critical areas to the Nigerians: the spirit world. In Kraft's words,

> Neither my anthropological nor my biblical and theological training had provided me with any constructive approaches to meet their felt need. The power of God to heal and deliver from demons was a frequent theme of the Nigerian leaders in their preaching. But we never demonstrated what we claimed in this area. So those we sought to reach were not very impressed with that part of our message. There seemed to be more visible power in their old ways

than in Christianity. As missionaries we had brought an essentially powerless message to a very power-conscious people.[1]

He saw demonic manifestations cast out through prayer, not psychology. He saw believers healed, not by technique but by authority. He saw spiritual warfare up close: raw, unsanitized, undeniable. And in that collision between intellectual control and supernatural reality, Kraft experienced what he later called his "second conversion."

He realized that the church he had known—the church of reason, ritual, and restraint—was missing the very power it professed to believe in. The tragedy wasn't that Americans didn't know how to do church. It was that we no longer knew how to be the church—the kind that commands attention in hell.

Kraft later concluded, "Spiritual power is the birthright of all Christians. Why are we Evangelicals not appropriating this part of our inheritance?"[2]

• •

The Spirit is the hinge of the whole story. Without him, the Christian life collapses into moral effort and intellectual agreement. With him, the story pivots into power—ordinary believers becoming conduits of heaven's fire.

• •

This chapter begins with Kraft's awakening for one reason: it is not unique. His story is our story, or it can be. Because like him, we have been trained by a system that subtly conditions us to distrust power, avoid the miraculous, and minimize the Spirit. And that's how Stockholm Syndrome becomes normal.

When the miraculous becomes mythical, when formation becomes therapeutic, when truth becomes optional, when the Spirit becomes embarrassing, the triangle collapses. And the church flatlines.

If we are to recover the fullness of kingdom life, we must start at the highest point: the apex of the Kingdom Triangle. Here the winds of Pentecost still roar, and the fire of God still falls. This is not a theological

---

1. Kraft, *Christianity with Power*, 4.
2. Kraft, *Christianity with Power*, 8.

checkpoint to acknowledge, but the catalytic center of New Testament Christianity.

A GEOMETRY OF POWER

This concept comes into clearer view in the following visual framework—figure 1, the Kingdom Triangle.

Figure 1   *Kingdom Triangle Diagram.* **Created by Steve W. Johnson, 2025.**

Notice the placement: the Spirit is not just one side among equals. He occupies the apex, the highest point, from which energy and structure flow downward to the mind and the soul. This is no accident. The downward arrows symbolize more than position; they reveal divine propulsion. The Spirit empowers the believer at the point of deepest need, transforming what is naturally limited into something supernaturally alive.

Now, geometry may not seem like a revival topic, but in this case, the angles matter. In geometry, a triangle is the simplest and strongest of all shapes. It is formed by three vertices—points where lines converge to create structure, strength, and stability. With three points and three connecting edges, the triangle forms a unified whole. Remove one vertex, and the structure collapses into a line or a single point.

But not all vertices serve the same purpose. One rises above the rest—the apex, the peak, the summit, the focal height where all direction and energy converge. The Kingdom Triangle operates on the same principle.

Spirit Apex

Its three vertices—a recovered Christian mind, a soul infused with shalom, and the empowering presence of the Holy Spirit—are all essential to its stability. Yet one vertex gives life to the rest: the Spirit Apex.

Before we can realign our lives and ministries around that apex, we must first understand the geometry of the Kingdom itself. Every line has meaning. Every connection matters. The way we order the points of the triangle determines whether it stands as a structure of strength or collapses into another two-dimensional diagram of forgotten faith. When the Spirit Apex is restored to its rightful place, the Kingdom Triangle becomes more than theory—it becomes a framework for revival.

This is the church in motion, the Stockdale Church, tested by fire but filled with force. This is what we were meant to be.

Without the Spirit, the mind stalls at insight and the soul falls short of shalom. But when power descends from above, the natural is transformed into the supernatural. Apart from Him, the triangle collapses—the renewed mind loses clarity, the resilient soul loses peace. The Spirit is not an accessory to the Christian life; He is its animating flame.

The early church understood this. They didn't begin their mission with strategy sessions or position papers. They began with a prayer meeting that shook the room (Acts 4:31). Jesus' final command wasn't to get organized; it was to wait in Jerusalem until they were clothed with power from on high (Luke 24:49). That power was not optional then, and it is not optional now.

The Spirit Apex is not a supplement—he is the source. Apart from him, the kingdom remains a concept. With him, it becomes a commission with power.

Revival doesn't begin with a strategy; it begins with power. And if we're serious about kingdom renewal, we must start where Jesus told his disciples to start: with the Spirit.

Kraft's story forces us to ask hard questions: Have we been building our ministries, our churches, or even our personal faith with the Spirit politely sidelined? Have we settled for theological correctness without supernatural authority?

If the Spirit Apex is the place where the Kingdom Triangle takes its shape and receives its force, then anything less is not just incomplete—it's powerless. The question is not whether we admire the early church's fire, but whether we will wait, pray, and contend until that same fire burns in us.

STOCKDALE PARADOX CHRISTIANITY

EMPOWERED FROM THE APEX: WHY PENTECOST WAS, AND STILL IS, NECESSARY

Early on, the disciples faced a profound dilemma. For three years they had walked with Jesus, not just listening to his teaching but witnessing firsthand the character, compassion, and authority with which he lived. They saw miracles. They heard divine wisdom. They watched him love the unlovable, confront evil, and live in constant communion with the Father. If anyone knew Jesus, they did.

But all of that came crashing down at the cross.

When Jesus was crucified and placed in a tomb, their hope collapsed with him. Though they had seen too much to fully doubt, they were still overwhelmed by fear. They barricaded themselves behind locked doors, afraid that they too might be hunted down and executed. Their heads held knowledge, but their hearts were fractured. They believed he was the Messiah, yet he was dead. The dissonance between what they knew and what they felt was paralyzing.

Then came resurrection.

On the evening of that day, Jesus appeared alive, scarred but triumphant. He showed them his wounds. Their fear gave way to joy. And in that moment of reunion, Jesus did something curious: he breathed on them and said, "Receive the Holy Spirit" (John 20:22). Immediately before that, he had commissioned them with kingdom purpose: "As the Father has sent Me, I also send you" (John 20:21). They were now his ambassadors. Sent ones. But something was still missing.

Because forty days later, Jesus gave them a very different instruction: "not to leave Jerusalem, but to wait for the Father's promise. . . . 'You will be baptized with the Holy Spirit not many days from now'" (Acts 1:4–5).

Wait a minute. Hadn't they already received the Holy Spirit in that upper room moment? Why the delay? Why the command to wait if the Spirit had already been given?

This is the apex principle at work.

What they had received in John 20 was the Spirit's indwelling presence, new birth, internal life, divine companionship. But what they still lacked was the Spirit's empowering presence: boldness, spiritual authority, and supernatural commissioning for mission. The breath of the risen Christ gave them regeneration. But Pentecost would give them fire. And fire was what they needed.

They didn't just need comfort—they needed courage. They didn't just need peace—they needed power. Babies are born with life, but not with strength. In the same way, the disciples had been born of the Spirit but had not yet been baptized in power. That baptism would give them what regeneration alone could not: holy boldness, prophetic clarity, miraculous authority, spiritual gifts, and an indomitable resolve to crash the gates of hell.

It is only after Pentecost that the Kingdom Triangle becomes fully energized. The apex ignites the entire framework. Mind, soul, and Spirit begin operating in supernatural harmony. What had once been fearful followers becomes a fearless church, demonstrating the gospel in word, deed, and undeniable power.

This wasn't optional for Jesus. It was foundational.

As Francis MacNutt observed,

> Jesus clearly prioritized things differently than we do today. His public ministry was not a seminar on ethics or a traveling lecture series—it was a Spirit-empowered demonstration of the kingdom. He taught, yes, but He also healed the sick, cast out demons, embraced outcasts, and restored the broken. This was His norm, not the exception. Miracles weren't rare interruptions of natural order; they were what life looked like when the Spirit ruled.[3]

And this Spirit-infused lifestyle wasn't just for Jesus.

He commissioned his followers to carry it forward. "I assure you," Jesus said, "the one who believes in Me will also do the works that I do. And he will do even greater works than these" (John 14:12). That wasn't metaphor. That was mandate. Jesus expected his disciples, not just the twelve but all who would believe, to become conduits of his kingdom, empowered from the apex, operating as Spirit-filled agents of renewal in a broken world. And that's the great reversal: what was once considered supernatural was now to become super-normative for the Spirit-filled believer.

THE UPPER ROOM MANDATE

Jesus' final command before his ascension was not a strategy session or a theological lecture. It was a mandate to wait (Acts 1:4). Before Peter preached, before Paul taught, before a single missionary was sent, the disciples were told to wait for power. This was not passive hesitation—it was

---

3. MacNutt, *Nearly Perfect Crime*, 47.

spiritual readiness. They were not being stalled. They were being staged for ignition.

•••••••••••••••••••••••••••••••••

What makes the church dangerous is not its size, strategy, or sophistication—but its surrender to the Spirit.

•••••••••••••••••••••••••••••••••

The upper room was not a delay tactic. It was the divine pattern. Pentecost was not a luxury. It was the launch. Every generation of disciples must pass through the "upper room." It is there, in surrender, in hunger, in expectation, that God lights the fire that the world cannot extinguish.

Just as the early disciples waited in the upper room until they were clothed with power from on high (Luke 24:49), so must we begin with power to proceed. Until the Spirit fires the ignition, nothing moves. He directs, coordinates, empowers, and completes the work. To attempt recovery or renovation without the Spirit is to try starting a vehicle without fuel, spark, or direction.

The Spirit is not a latecomer to the church's strategy. He is the strategy. Jesus himself, though fully divine, chose to live and minister under the anointing of the Spirit (Luke 4:1, 18; Acts 10:38). Before his followers could teach, preach, disciple, or heal, they had to wait because mission without power is motion without momentum.

The tragedy is that many modern believers have never had their own Pentecost. They are followers of Jesus in name and belief, but have not yet been clothed with power from on high. They are sincere but stalled, committed but disconnected. And the invitation remains open: "If you then, who are evil, know how to give good gifts to your children, how much more will the heavenly Father give the Holy Spirit to those who ask Him?" (Luke 11:13).

This passage has confused many believers. But, as discussed in the previous section, we have the Holy Spirit at regeneration. That is why the church did not begin in Acts 2; it began in John 20:22, when Jesus breathed on his disciples and said, "Receive the Holy Spirit." So, what then is Jesus referring to here in Luke 11 and Acts 1?

The answer is clear: while we receive the Holy Spirit at conversion as seal, indwelling presence, and identity marker, there remains a distinct infilling with power, authority, and commissioning. Just as the disciples received the Spirit in John 20, they were still told to wait for the promised empowerment in Acts 1.

This isn't contradiction; it's completion. It's one thing to have the engine installed; it's another thing to turn the key and feel the combustion. Do you want to be a part of God's power team? Then ask the Father for the Spirit to connect the triangle—not to merely dwell, but to ignite. He will gladly do it. He delights to empower. He longs to launch you into the supernatural life you were always meant to live.

Gordon Fee wrote, "God's empowering presence is the defining mark of New Testament Christianity."[4] And yet, that defining mark has been functionally erased. We know the creeds. We affirm the doctrines. But we lack the combustion. The early church waited for the flame. We have often settled for the form.

But it doesn't have to remain this way. The Spirit's power is not a relic of the past. He is present and eager to fill, again and again, those who hunger for more. This isn't about emotional highs or charismatic extremes. It's about the presence of God taking up residence in the human heart with transformative force.

This is your moment. Ask him. Invite him. Wait for him. The upper room was not a detour. It was the doorway. Pentecost was not a bonus. It was the beginning. Every disciple who would carry fire into the world must first sit in surrender and hunger and expectation, just like they did: together, praying, waiting for the flame that would ignite the church.

This is the upper room mandate.

And when the fire falls, don't look back.

Because when the Spirit fills a life, the real journey begins.

THE OVERLOOKED GOD

For much of modern church history, the Holy Spirit has been treated like the quiet cousin of the Trinity—present, but often politely ignored. While we exalt the Father as Creator and the Son as Redeemer, the Spirit, who is equally God, is frequently relegated to symbolic language or mystical mystery. Many believers are uncertain about how to engage the Spirit, and many pastors avoid the topic altogether for fear of controversy or excess.

The result is a theological imbalance. We affirm the creeds but sidestep the combustion. We honor the Father and preach the Son, but

4. Fee, *God's Empowering Presence*, 6.

we mumble about the Spirit. And when we do, we often reduce him to an inner feeling or a moment of inspiration, rather than the living, empowering Person of the Godhead.

This isn't just bad theology—it's dangerous. Because if the Spirit is simply an inner feeling, he cannot be sought. If he is only an idea, he cannot be obeyed. And if he is not a Person, he cannot be known.

Sadly, this isn't just a theoretical problem. A Barna study found that nearly six in ten born-again Christians believe the Holy Spirit is merely a symbol of God's power or presence—not a living person. That's 60 percent. Only about three in ten affirmed the Spirit as a distinct person of the Trinity.[5] Think about the ramifications of that worldview construct. If that's what the church believes, it's no wonder we struggle to walk in power. You can't follow a symbol. You can't be led by a metaphor. And you certainly can't be filled by something you don't believe is real.

Jack Deere, once a staunch cessationist and professor at Dallas Theological Seminary, underwent a personal awakening. His own reading of Scripture began to contradict the doctrine he had been trained to teach. He recounts, "There is not a single verse in the New Testament that teaches the gifts of the Spirit would cease before Christ's return. In fact, every indication is that they are normal for the entire church age."[6]

Similarly, Craig Keener, in his exhaustive two-volume work *Miracles*, affirms that "there is not one shred of biblical evidence that the spiritual gifts were ever meant to cease with the apostolic age."[7] His research highlights global testimonies of healings and miracles as consistent with the biblical narrative.

Francis MacNutt, a pioneer in the Catholic Charismatic Renewal, wrote, "The gifts never left; we just stopped using them. We became content with theological precision and lost our appetite for divine power."[8]

These voices echo the same conclusion: the suppression of the Spirit's power was not God's idea. It was ours.

Pentecostal scholars have affirmed this as well, not as a denominational defense but as a deeply biblical conviction. Their research, shaped by both rigorous scholarship and lived experience, pushes back against the sterilized theology that has domesticated the Spirit.

---

5. Barna, *Think Like Jesus*, 89.
6. Deere, *Surprised by the Power*, 45.
7. Keener, *Miracles*, 1:775.
8. MacNutt, *Healing Reawakening*, 44.

Pentecostal theologian, author, and professor Cheryl Bridges Johns, reflecting on the crisis of modern spirituality, warns that in much of the twenty-first-century church, "the silence of the Bible is deafening. . . . It does not haunt us, filling our days with images and stories. . . . It is a text that has been stripped of its power . . . a disenchanted text."[9] In such an environment, where the Spirit is marginalized, we are left with a form of Christianity that may be intellectually sharp but is often spiritually sterile. The miraculous becomes mythical. The word becomes weightless. And the church, though informed, becomes impotent.

Amos Yong, a leading Pentecostal theologian and dean of the School of Mission and Theology at Fuller Theological Seminary, extends this critique by showing how the Spirit is not only the engine of mission but the grounding presence of theological thought itself. He writes, "The Spirit is not just the power of missions but the presence who gives rise to the very possibility of theology itself."[10]

Frank Macchia, a distinguished Pentecostal theologian and professor of systematic theology at Vanguard University, brings the argument home by insisting that Pentecost is not peripheral to Christian identity—it is the drama. "Pentecost represents not a side story, but the central drama of Christian identity and mission."[11]

Together, these voices do not merely call for balance; they call for biblical fidelity. The gifts and presence of the Spirit are not optional expressions. They are essential manifestations of New Testament life, and without them, the church operates in deficit.

This understanding is not new. The early church fathers bore witness to the Spirit's work as a present and ongoing force. Irenaeus of Lyons, writing in the second century, declared, "For some do certainly drive out devils, so that those who have been cleansed from evil spirits frequently both believe in Christ and join themselves to the Church."[12]

Justin Martyr, also testified, "For the prophetical gifts remain with us, even to the present time."[13] These early leaders did not view the Spirit's gifts as temporary or exceptional; they were the expected norm for Christian life.

---

9. Bridges Johns, *Re-Enchanting the Text*, 12–13.
10. Yong, *Spirit Poured Out*, 17.
11. Macchia, *Baptized in the Spirit*, 15.
12. Irenaeus, *Against Heresies* 2.32.4 (Ante-Nicene Fathers 1:409).
13. Justin Martyr, *Dialogue with Trypho* 82.1 (Falls, 240).

The historical witness affirms what Scripture reveals and what contemporary theologians are recovering: the Spirit's power is not a past-tense phenomenon. It is the present-tense engine of the church.

When believers begin to see the Spirit not as a metaphor but as a Person who empowers and equips, the entire texture of Christian life changes. Theology becomes expectation. Worship becomes encounter. Mission becomes supernatural. To ignore him is not humility. It's disobedience. And to welcome him is not fanaticism. It's loyalty.

The church does not need more clever strategies. It needs more Spirit-filled saints. That begins by recovering a right view of the Spirit, not as a theological accessory but as the living power of God active in the church today.

HDJL—HOW DID JESUS LIVE?

Before we apply the triangle as our framework for discipleship, we must understand how it was first embodied in the life of Jesus. The Kingdom Triangle is not a clever construct. It is a reflection of how our Savior lived—entirely empowered by the Spirit, grounded in the truth, and formed in deep wholeness.

Jesus was conceived by the Spirit (Luke 1:35), baptized in the Spirit (Luke 3:22), led by the Spirit (Luke 4:1), and ministered in the power of the Spirit (Luke 4:14). Everything he said, everything he did, and everything he accomplished flowed through the Spirit's presence in and upon him.

As Peter later summarized, "God anointed Jesus of Nazareth with the Holy Spirit and with power, and . . . He went about doing good and healing all who were under the tyranny of the Devil, because God was with Him" (Acts 10:38).

Jesus didn't perform miracles by virtue of his divinity. He lived as the Spirit-anointed Son, demonstrating what a life fully yielded to God looks like. He didn't skip the triangle, he modeled it.

- He taught with clarity and authority—the recovered mind (Luke 4:32).
- He withdrew to pray and practiced holy rhythms—the renovated soul (Mark 1:35).
- He healed, delivered, and empowered others—the restored Spirit power (Luke 5:17).

This is not just Christology. It is discipleship 101. Jesus' way of life was never meant to be admired from a distance. It was meant to be replicated by his followers, in the same Spirit, with the same access, and for the same mission.

The church that forgets how Jesus lived will inevitably reduce the Christian life to moral aspiration or doctrinal assent. But when we follow him into the triangle, when we live HDJL, we step into the pattern he laid down for us.

Let us not only worship Jesus as Lord. Let us also walk as he walked, filled with the Spirit, anchored in truth, and formed into wholeness. The church was never meant to be a stationary exhibit of theological design. It was created to move. To roar. To crush the gates of hell. But only when all three vertices of the Kingdom Triangle are fully engaged—the mind, the soul, and the Spirit—can it move with divine force.

Recovering the Christian mind equips us to discern and declare the truth in a world allergic to certainty. Renovating the soul restores our identity, making us whole humans who carry the character of Christ into a fractured world. But without the Spirit's ignition, even the sharpest mind and the strongest soul stall in place.

We don't just need right ideas. We don't just need deep formation. We need power: holy, unpredictable, culture-defying, devil-displacing power. The kind that made Pharisees tremble, cities stir, and demons beg for mercy. That kind of power only flows through a triangle that has been rewired and reconnected.

This is the geometry of the kingdom, not as theory but as strategy. The mind clarifies. The soul anchors. The Spirit activates. Each depends on the others. Each completes the others. Without one, the shape collapses. Without the Spirit, it's a flat line, not a three-vertex powerful triangle! But with the full triangle engaged, the church becomes something terrifying to the gates of hell: intelligent, whole, and supernaturally alive.

This is the church in motion—the Stockdale Church, tested by fire but filled with force. This is what we were meant to be.

THE TRIANGLE AS TACTICAL THEOLOGY

Why a triangle? Why not a square, or a circle, or a linear path? Because a triangle is the most elemental geometric shape capable of bearing weight and maintaining stability. Architects and engineers use triangles because of their unique ability to distribute pressure evenly. Remove one point and the entire structure fails. Theologically, the Kingdom Triangle operates the same way.

J. P. Moreland didn't invent the shape; he rediscovered a biblical pattern. The Christian life, when lived in its full New Testament dynamic, pulses with these three coordinates: right thinking, deep being, and supernatural doing. It is how Jesus lived. He taught with intellectual clarity (mind), walked in relational wholeness (soul), and ministered in divine power (Spirit). He modeled the triangle before J. P. ever gave it a name.

We see this trifold design emerge again and again in Scripture:

- Paul prays for believers to be "transformed by the renewing of your mind" (Rom 12:2),
- That they would be "sanctified entirely—spirit, soul, and body" (1 Thess 5:23),
- And that their faith would rest not on "human wisdom, but on the power of God" (1 Cor 2:5).

The triangle is not a schematic for scholars. It is tactical theology—a field-ready formation for Christians engaged in a war of ideologies, temptations, and principalities. When the triangle is intact, the believer becomes sturdy, discerning, and courageous.

However, the church's default mode tends to be reductionist. Intellectual traditions emphasize orthodoxy while suppressing the supernatural. Charismatic movements elevate the Spirit while neglecting disciplined formation. Activist churches form the soul around causes without deeply renewing the mind. The result? Lopsided Christianity: dynamic but shallow, informed but inactive, passionate but naïve.

But the triangle is a call back to balance and boldness. It is not an abstract model to admire; it is a theological chassis meant to move. It holds the tension of rigor, resilience, and revelation. It prevents over-specialization and forces us to see discipleship as a holistic, Spirit-driven formation strategy.

In a time when the church is fragmented and the culture is fracturing, we need this tactical geometry more than ever. But it must be a balanced triangle, not a distorted one.

The church often favors one side over the others, creating malformed triangles: an isosceles triangle overly weighted on intellect and formation but lacking supernatural activation; or a scalene triangle driven by sporadic experiences of the Spirit with shallow discipleship and little theological clarity. These are not Kingdom Triangles. They are theological deformities.

Only the equilateral triangle, where all three vertices are engaged in equal measure—truth, formation, and power—can hold kingdom weight and generate forward motion. That's when the church becomes not just resilient but dangerous to the gates of hell. This is the shape of kingdom resistance. This is how we build a people who cannot be shaken.

WHAT HAPPENS WITHOUT THE SPIRIT

When the Spirit is sidelined, the consequences are not merely spiritual; they are theological, pastoral, and missional.

Theological Outcomes

We end up with theology without transformation. Doctrine becomes data. Biblical truth is studied like a fossil: admired but lifeless. The Spirit, the one who leads us into all truth (John 16:13), is reduced to a theological footnote. Without him, Christianity becomes a philosophy class: intellectually rigorous but spiritually inert.

Pastoral Outcomes

The pulpit shifts from conviction to comfort. Instead of inviting people into the fire of God's presence, we settle for climate-controlled religion. Conviction gives way to careful neutrality. Instead of leading people into surrender, we coach them into safety. We avoid the discomfort of the Spirit in favor of predictable, manageable faith.

Missional Outcomes

Our activism lacks authority. We campaign for justice but neglect the power that drives it. We do outreach without outflow. Without the Spirit, our compassion becomes charity and our mission becomes marketing. We become a lifeboat with no oars: afloat, but directionless. Or a beautiful house with no electricity: impressive, but powerless.

This is not just a loss of experience; it is a collapse of effectiveness. The church cannot accomplish a supernatural mission with natural means. Without the Spirit, our ministries become motion without movement, form without fire. This is why reengaging the Spirit is not optional. It is essential. Because without him, we are left with elegant theology, polished souls, and utterly no power.

THE PINNACLE OF PRESENCE: WHY THE SPIRIT MUST LEAD

We opened this chapter with Charles Kraft's unsettling experience in Nigeria. Armed with education, cultural sensitivity, and theological precision, Kraft and his wife sincerely believed they were ready. But what they lacked was what the people most needed—the manifest power of the Holy Spirit. Kraft later confessed that while they had brought the gospel in word, they had not brought it in power.

That realization didn't just challenge his theology—it broke it wide open. It revealed how deeply the Western church had filtered out the supernatural, leaving behind a gospel of reason, ritual, and restraint. Kraft's "second conversion" was not about doctrine; it was about rediscovering the Spirit as the indispensable, present-tense power for ministry. What he witnessed overseas exposed what had been quietly lost at home.

And so we're left with a sobering truth: our greatest deficiency is not strategy, sincerity, or structure. It's the absence of power.

Strategy may keep the machinery running, but only the Spirit makes the mission unstoppable. Until the church hungers more for fire than formulas, we will remain busy but barren.

The Holy Spirit is not optional. He is the apex, the ignition point of kingdom life. He alone transforms theory into fire. He alone connects the mind and soul to the mission of God in power. And he is not reluctant. He is ready.

But the surge does not begin in motion. It begins in stillness. In hunger. In surrender. In waiting. Like the disciples in the upper room, like Kraft

Spirit Apex

in the villages of Nigeria, we must come to the end of ourselves, our cleverness, our confidence, our control, and say, "Come, Holy Spirit."

This chapter is not just about balance—it's about priority. The Spirit is the pinnacle of presence. He is the apex of divine encounter, the summit from which all true Christian living flows. But the Spirit doesn't bypass the mind or override the will. He fills what we submit. He empowers what we surrender. He sets ablaze what we offer on the altar.

To thrive in this kingdom life, then, is to recognize that the Spirit must lead. Not as a last resort, not as a theological footnote, but as the commanding presence that guides the mind, forms the soul, and advances the mission of God through power, truth, and love.

The Spirit Apex is not a metaphor. It is the lived reality of kingdom transformation. So if we are to recover the dynamic life God intended, we must start not at the base, but at the pinnacle. Because the next move of God will not bypass the mind. It will reclaim it.

We now turn to the second vertex of the triangle: the recovered Christian mind—because too many Christians have lost theirs.

CHAPTER 5

Christians Have Lost Their Minds!

The collision between a Christian mind and a solidly earthbound culture ought to be a violent one.

—Harry Blamires, *The Christian Mind*

Our minds are not neutral or passive; they are battlegrounds. In every moment, they are either being shaped by the truth of God or seduced by the narratives of culture. They are not bystanders in the fight for faith—they are the front lines. There is no such thing as a spiritually disengaged mind. Every thought we entertain is either inching us toward transformation or dragging us toward conformity.

This chapter doesn't begin with reflection; it begins with resistance. In this age, knowing is warfare. If we don't fight for our minds, we will lose them by default.

The battle for the Christian mind is not about making the church smarter; it's about making the church stronger. It's not merely a call to intellectualism but to resilience, clarity, and conviction in a world bent on confusion. That's why the second vertex of the Kingdom Triangle is the recovery of a biblically grounded, Spirit-empowered epistemology, a way of knowing infused with heaven's perspective.

As J. P. Moreland explains, "To think Christianly is not to think about Christian things. It is to think about everything from a Christian point of view."[1] This isn't about compartmentalized religious thought; it's about a

---

1. Moreland, *Kingdom Triangle*, 94.

worldview overhaul. It's the difference between having Christian opinions and cultivating a mind fully surrendered to Christ's truth in every domain of life.

We are not here to decorate our minds with Christian slogans. We are here to salvage them into strongholds of truth. Stockholm Christianity has turned the mind into a sponge, absorbing culture, echoing slogans, parroting feelings. But a recovered Christian mind is not soft; it is sharp. Not reactive, but resilient. Not anxious, but anchored.

• •

The Christian mind is not a luxury—it is a lifeline. To abandon it is to surrender before the battle begins, leaving the church reactive, fragile, and easily swayed by the loudest cultural voice.

• •

THE FULL FORCE OF THE ASSAULT

In the introduction of his short diatribe, *Letter to a Christian Nation*, atheist Sam Harris opens with a chilling statement of purpose: "I have set out to demolish the intellectual and moral pretensions of Christianity in its most committed forms."[2]

Harris believes the vast majority of Christians are not thinkers and therefore cannot produce even the most rudimentary apologetic or reasons for faith, which, sadly, may be accurate for far too many believers. Throughout his book, he openly mocks Christians as unintelligent, unable to defend their own convictions.

Yet in a moment of rare intellectual candor, Harris admits there is the possibility he could be wrong. He acknowledges that either the Bible is God's word, or it isn't. Jesus is either the one true pathway to salvation, or he's not. To be a Christian, Harris concedes, is to believe all other religions are profoundly mistaken. And if the Bible is true, then by rejecting God he fully expects to face the consequences.

Right before launching into his relentless attack, he writes, "If the basic doctrine of Christianity is correct, I have misused my life in the worst conceivable way. I admit this without a single caveat. The fact that my continuous and public rejection of Christianity does not worry me in the least

---

2. Harris, *Letter to a Christian Nation*, ix.

should suggest to you just how inadequate I think your reasons for being a Christian are."[3]

Though Harris concedes he could be wrong, his words remain a blistering indictment of Christians' lack of intellectual depth. Which leaves us with the pressing question: How are we to stand in a culture that declares either truth is only what science defines or that no truth exists at all?

Into this fog of confusion, Jesus speaks with startling clarity: "You will know the truth, and the truth will set you free" (John 8:32). The Greek word for "know" here points to experiential knowledge. Jesus insists truth is not merely an abstract proposition—it can be known, encountered, and lived. And that truth liberates.

So we are faced with a choice: either buy into the reigning worldviews that deny objective reality, or trust Jesus when he says absolute truth exists and is knowable. If loving God with all our mind is the greatest commandment, then we cannot afford mental passivity. We must engage with our brains.

Before we turn to Paul's bold imperative in Rom 12:2, let's pause for a story, a true account that shows, in living color, why the Christian mind matters and why it desperately needs recovery. In *Kingdom Triangle*, Moreland recounts the experience of Dr. Helen Roseveare, a medical missionary in Zaire.[4]

A young mother had given birth and died, leaving behind her newborn and a two-year-old sister. Though in equatorial Africa, the nights were cold and the baby needed warmth to survive. But the orphanage's last hot water bottle had burst. That afternoon, a ten-year-old girl named Ruth prayed boldly—not just for a water bottle, but for a doll to comfort the baby. "God, it'll be no good tomorrow, the baby will be dead. Please send it this afternoon," she said.

Dr. Roseveare was stunned. No parcel had arrived in four years, and who would send a hot water bottle to central Africa? But that same afternoon, a package arrived. As the orphanage children gathered around, Dr. Roseveare began opening the parcel, pulling out useful supplies for the clinic and orphanage. She reached her hand into the box again—and the shape was unmistakable. A brand new hot water bottle. Tears welled up in her eyes as she held it in disbelief. She later confessed, "I had not asked God for it; I had not believed that He could."

---

3. Harris, *Letter to a Christian Nation*, 6.
4. Moreland, *Kingdom Triangle*, 165–66.

Ruth, sitting in the front row of the children, cried out with joy, "If God has sent the bottle, He must have sent the dolly too!" She rummaged further down, and there it was—a small, beautifully dressed doll. Her eyes sparkled. She had never doubted. Looking up at Dr. Roseveare, she asked, "Can I go over with you and give this dolly to that little girl, so she'll know that Jesus really loves her?"

That parcel had been in the mail for five whole months, packed by Dr. Roseveare's former Sunday school class whose leader had felt prompted by God to include a hot water bottle—despite the seeming absurdity of sending one to the equator. Before Ruth prayed, before the baby was born, and before the young mother had died, the parcel was already on its way. And the specific request by Ruth for a dolly—so that the little girl would know that Jesus loved her—was met with divine precision. That's the faith of a child met by the answer of a God who sees, cares, and responds.

Depending on your worldview, you'll process this story very differently. If God is distant or uninvolved, it will seem improbable—maybe even offensive. But if God is present and active, then this account is not strange at all; it's a vivid reminder that he delights to answer prayer with precision.

So what do we make of it? The naturalist shrugs it off as coincidence or fabrication. The postmodernist reduces it to a private truth meaningful only to Ruth and Dr. Roseveare. The Christian, however, must wrestle—either to marvel at God's care or to ask why such interventions seem absent in their own life.

And that wrestling reveals more than just opinion; it exposes the lens through which we see all of reality. Our worldview is not window dressing; it is the framework that shapes how we interpret every event, every expectation, and every act of God. Which is why Paul insists in Rom 12:2 that we cannot afford to be conformed to this world's categories of thought—we must be transformed by the renewing of our minds.

STOCKDALE THINKING: THE RENEWED MIND IN THE HEAT OF BATTLE

Romans 12:2 issues a bold imperative: "Do not be conformed to this age, but be transformed by the renewing of your mind." This verse stands as a hinge between salvation and sanctification, a call for transformation not merely of behavior, but of cognition. The word "conformed" here reflects the Stockholm dynamic: a passive assimilation to the surrounding culture, a subconscious loyalty to captors of the mind like naturalism, postmodernism, and comfort. In contrast, "transformed" is the path of the Stockdale Christian—one who embraces brutal truth, clings to eternal hope, and experiences a Spirit-empowered mental metamorphosis.

And here is the game changer: the "renewing of your mind." But how does that happen? Reading, studying, and meditating all help, yet if left to human effort alone, they fall short. True renewal comes not from striving, but from surrender. As Jesus said in Luke 9:23, "If anyone wants to come with Me, he must deny himself, take up his cross daily, and follow Me." Denying. Dying. Following. This is the gateway to transformation. A Spirit-renewed mind is the result of a Spirit-surrendered life.

Yet most Christians, if honest, remain tethered to old patterns of thinking, not because they lack desire but because they lack power. The challenge is not merely intellectual; it is spiritual. We long to think rightly but find ourselves stuck in mental habits that no longer serve the kingdom. The war for the mind is relentless, and without the Spirit's power, we are overrun.

This is why the Spirit Apex is essential. Transformation begins at the top of the triangle: with Spirit baptism and empowerment. Without the Spirit's presence, the Christian mind cannot be renewed. Left to itself, the natural mind is enslaved by sin, hostile to God, and incapable of pleasing him (Rom 8:7–8). Paul's call in Rom 12:2 is not a summons to try harder but an invitation to surrender deeper. Only then can the depraved mind be remade, and only then can the renewed mind emerge as ground reclaimed by the Spirit.

What follows is an honest look at how that ground was lost: the ideologies that sabotaged the Christian mind, the seductions that dulled it, and the cultural captivity that compromised it. But diagnosis is not the final word. If the enemy has built strongholds, the Spirit has also forged weapons.

The journey ahead traces not just recovery but revolution—where the Spirit brings clarity to confusion, conviction to compromise, and boldness to retreat. This is more than a call to better thinking; it is a summons to Spirit-shaped transformation. If we will face the brutal truth, confront our condition, and fully yield our thoughts to His renovating power, transformation will not be wishful—it will be inevitable. The time has come to think differently: sharply, courageously, and with the clarity only heaven can provide.

CHRISTIANS HAVE LOST THEIR MINDS!

THE DEPRAVITY OF THE NATURAL MIND

The Scriptures are clear: the mind apart from God is not neutral ground. It is darkened in its understanding (Eph 4:18) and incapable of discerning the things of the Spirit (1 Cor 2:14).

Paul outlines the descent of the natural mind in Rom 1:21–23:

> For though they knew God, they did not glorify Him as God or show gratitude. Instead, their thinking became nonsense, and their senseless minds were darkened. Claiming to be wise, they became fools and exchanged the glory of the immortal God for images resembling mortal man, birds, four-footed animals, and reptiles.

The result was not just moral degradation but intellectual depravity. "God delivered them over to a worthless mind to do what is morally wrong" (Rom 1:28).

Left to itself, the human mind does not drift toward truth—it decays into rebellion. Paul just made it clear, that this fleshly mindset is not merely ignorant but actively hostile to God. Left unchecked, it resists his truth and refuses his law, making genuine transformation impossible without the Spirit's intervention.

The evidence of this depravity is seen all around us. From the rise of relativism that denies any objective truth, to scientism that insists only the material can be real, to cynicism that scoffs at faith as childish and delusional. The world is not shy about ridiculing belief in God. Cultural critics like comedian George Carlin reduce Christianity to mockery, painting it as nothing more than superstition enforced by threats of eternal punishment.[5] Such caricatures land with power in a generation largely untrained to defend their faith.

The result is predictable: many believers, lacking intellectual discipleship, retreat into a privatized faith that cannot withstand scrutiny. To the watching world, Christians appear emotionally sincere but intellectually unserious. And until the church recovers a Spirit-renewed mind, it will continue to confirm the caricature rather than confront it.

CHRISTIANS HAVE LOST THEIR MINDS

Mark Noll, in his landmark book *The Scandal of the Evangelical Mind*, famously wrote, "The scandal of the evangelical mind is that there is not

---

5. Carlin, *You Are All Diseased*.

much of an evangelical mind."[6] His point was blunt: Evangelicals have largely abandoned the task of rigorous intellectual engagement with culture, truth, and theology. We have traded thinking for feeling, discernment for experience, and truth for pragmatism.

Noll's critique echoes a much older warning. Hosea 4:6 declares, "My people are destroyed for lack of knowledge." Notice it does not say for lack of faith. Knowledge is the foundation upon which genuine faith rests. Without knowledge, faith collapses into mere sentiment. As Francis Schaeffer confirmed, the crisis in the modern church is not a lack of zeal but a lack of truth and understanding.[7]

Charles H. Malik, former Lebanese ambassador to the United States, made the same case in his 1980 address at the dedication of the Billy Graham Center at Wheaton College. "The problem is not only to win souls but to save minds. If you win the whole world and lose the mind of the world, you will soon discover you have not won the world. Indeed it may turn out you have actually lost the world. . . . I must be frank with you: The greatest danger besetting American evangelical Christianity is the danger of anti-intellectualism."[8]

Malik was not alone. Os Guinness, in his book *Fit Bodies, Fat Minds*, argues that the church's failure stems directly from its lack of a distinctly Christian mind. He describes this condition as a ghost mind. In the nineteenth century, many towns in the American West were abandoned, becoming ghost towns.[9] Likewise, many believers today inhabit faith with the hollowed-out shells of minds never trained to think Christianly.

••••••••••••••••••••••••••••••

A faith that cannot think will never stand. When the church forfeits the life of the mind, it concedes the cultural battlefield to unbelief and confirms the caricature of Christianity as shallow and irrelevant.

••••••••••••••••••••••••••••••

6. Noll, *Scandal of the Evangelical Mind*, 3.
7. Schaeffer, *Great Evangelical Disaster*, 38.
8. Malik, "Two Tasks," 294.
9. Guinness, *Fit Bodies, Fat Minds*, 14.

Add to this the influence of Hollywood, where theology is replaced by therapy. Brad Pitt once said, "When I got un-tethered from the comfort of religion, it wasn't a loss of faith for me, it was a discovery of self."[10] In our entertainment-saturated culture, Pitt's narcissism is the new orthodoxy. Faith is rebranded as self-expression. Church becomes self-help. And spiritual formation is exchanged for personality curation. As long as you feel spiritual, the culture applauds. But the mind surrendered to Christ doesn't seek applause—it seeks truth. That's the difference between cultural affirmation and kingdom transformation. And, that is why the natural mind is in desperate need of Spirit renovation and transformation.

TEMPTATION, DOUBT, AND UNBELIEF: THE CRACK IN THE MIND

But this loss of theological clarity doesn't begin with culture; it begins with a crack in the mind. Like Eve in the garden, temptation begins with a simple question: "Did God really say?" (Gen 3:1). The enemy doesn't need to dismantle belief entirely—just insert doubt. And doubt, when allowed to linger, becomes fertile soil for deception.

James explains the process for us in chapter 1, verses 14–15: "But each person is tempted when he is drawn away and enticed by his own evil desires. Then after desire has conceived, it gives birth to sin, and when sin is fully grown, it gives birth to death."

James makes it clear that temptation is not sin—but it is the baited hook. It works through our fleshly evil desires. What bait does the enemy throw out there to get your attention? It is something you already have a weakness toward. He appeals to your appetites.

But there is more going on here than meets the eye. The enemy knows which bait or lure to pull out of his tackle box that will appeal to your weaknesses. He appeals to your dopamine system.

Dopamine is a neurotransmitter, a chemical messenger in the brain that plays a central role in reward, motivation, and the experience of pleasure. When we anticipate something pleasurable, dopamine is released in anticipation of the reward. The enemy knows very well what raises your dopamine levels. Research shows that dopamine levels are actually higher

---

10. Rader, "Brad Pitt," 7.

in the desire, contemplation, and fantasizing state than they are in the actual participation stage.[11]

This makes the mind highly susceptible to temptation because even contemplating sin can trigger a flood of dopamine, creating a powerful draw toward indulgence. The enemy capitalizes on this design, inserting counterfeit commercials into our mental feed that promise fulfillment but lead to captivity. It distorts God's design for joy and satisfaction and replaces it with hollow, flesh-driven substitutes meant to hijack our thinking and enslave our will.

The battlefield is the mind. As believers, we face a daily barrage of seductive lies (see John 10:10). Evangelist and author, Joyce Meyer, underscores this reality: "Satan knows that if he can defeat us in our mind, he can defeat us in our experience. That's why it is so important that we not lose heart, grow weary and faint."[12] The enemy interrupts our routines with temptation, not merely to make us fall but to make us question. Temptation, when not resisted, leads to doubt. Doubt, left unattended, erodes trust. And trust lost, if not restored, becomes full-grown unbelief.

The answer isn't suppression—but submission. Freedom isn't found in denying every pleasure, but in redirecting our desires to their true source.

Our sinful natures want to be pandered to. They resist the Spirit and must be brought under submission. That is why the renewed mind is not merely informed—it must be surrendered. The mind, left unchecked, will rationalize rebellion. But a mind under the lordship of Christ can discern between the whisper of the serpent and the word of the Lord.

But here's the good news: God designed our dopamine systems. They are not accidental. They were meant to enhance joy, deepen satisfaction, and amplify the experience of his goodness. Sin has hijacked this design, offering counterfeit pleasures that never truly satisfy. But when we humble ourselves and submit to the guiding and directing of the Holy Spirit, something shifts. Our desires are rewired. Our pleasures are sanctified. The joy, peace, and fulfillment we begin to experience surpass anything the world can offer. It's not about dulling desire; it's about discovering its truest and highest expression in communion with God.

---

11. Weinschenk, "Dopamine Seekers."
12. Meyer, *Battlefield of the Mind*, 16.

WORLDVIEW SABOTAGE: NATURALISM AND POSTMODERNISM

This erosion of the Christian mind is not accidental—it's strategic. There is a demonic war being waged against biblical thinking. From kindergarten classrooms to university lecture halls, an anti-biblical agenda is being normalized, celebrated, and enforced. Liberal indoctrination doesn't just teach students how to think; it conditions them what to think. Critical thinking is replaced by cultural conformity. Questioning progressive orthodoxy is treated as heresy.

This is not just theory—it's reality. According to internal research from the Assemblies of God and studies cited by Barna, as many as 66 percent of Assemblies of God high school students lose their faith within four years at a secular university.[13] These aren't just statistics—they're sons and daughters, future pastors and missionaries, being swallowed by systems designed to dismantle their convictions.

While there are countless worldview options in the cultural marketplace, two stand out as dominant influencers behind this sabotage: scientific naturalism and postmodern relativism. These two have ransacked the Christian mind.

Naturalism asserts that all that exists is matter and energy: no soul, no God, no afterlife. It is the belief that everything can and must be explained solely through physical processes, without recourse to divine purpose or supernatural intervention. Under naturalism, humans are not image-bearers but accidents of biology. Life has no intrinsic meaning—only what we invent. In this framework, prayer is dismissed as superstition, and faith is ridiculed as a blind leap into the irrational.

This worldview aggressively attacks biblical Christianity because it refuses to tolerate any truth claim that cannot be measured under a microscope or tested in a laboratory. Faith, under this regime, is not viewed as trust rooted in evidence; it is treated as gullibility. Naturalism strips away wonder, silences transcendence, and presents a disenchanted cosmos where only atoms and energy exist.

Atheist astrophysicist Carl Sagan, summarizing this despair, declared, "Our planet is a lonely speck in the great enveloping cosmic dark.... In all this vastness, there is no hint that help will come from elsewhere to save us

---

13. Elmore, *Generation iY*, 89–91.

from ourselves."[14] That is not just science—it's a creed of despair disguised as objectivity.

To be clear, science is a wonderful and necessary discipline. It has enabled technological breakthroughs, medical advancements, and a deeper appreciation for the created order. But science, for all its power, is not equipped to construct a complete worldview. You cannot peer into a microscope or telescope and deduce the meaning of life, the reality of consciousness, or the existence of moral truth. Science can describe how things work, but it cannot explain why we exist. It cannot account for teleology, our ultimate purpose, or the transcendent longing in every human heart.

History reminds us that many of the greatest scientific minds were also devout theists. Newton, Copernicus, and Galileo didn't study the cosmos to escape God—they studied it to understand the wonder of his design. To them, science was an act of worship, a way of unveiling the glory of God in the heavens. The problem today is not science itself, but scientism: the belief that science is the only path to truth, which ironically cannot be proven by science itself.

Postmodernism, by contrast, is the philosophical antithesis of naturalism. Whereas naturalism insists that only what is scientifically measurable is real, postmodernism throws out all measuring sticks. It denies the existence of objective truth altogether, insisting instead that reality is whatever you make it. Truth becomes personal. Morality becomes relative. Identity becomes self-authored.

Postmodernity preaches, "Live your truth." It embraces the Pepsi-coined ethic: "Live for now." It dismantles all moral boundaries and replaces them with a fluid, feelings-first framework in which no one can tell anyone else they are wrong. The only remaining sin is making moral judgments. That's why biblical Christianity appears so archaic and offensive to this culture—it dares to assert that there are standards, absolutes, and a righteous Judge. Postmodernism may appear tolerant on the surface, but it ultimately tolerates everything except the lordship of Christ.

These twin ideologies—one scientific, the other social—are certainly not bedfellows. They disagree on origins, meaning, and metaphysics. But they share a common goal: to deconstruct reality and jettison any hope in a Designer who created humanity with great love and purpose. The tragedy is not only that this indoctrination dominates public education from kindergarten to university, but that it has infiltrated Christian universities and

---

14. Sagan, *Pale Blue Dot*, 9.

seminaries as well. Many pastors in pulpits today have literally lost their minds, spewing false doctrines and baptizing secular systems of belief with biblical language. Is it any wonder that the church has no power to confront culture? It has been captured by culture.

A MIND WORTH SAVING: JESUS AND THE RECOVERED MIND

Jesus raised the intellectual stakes when he amended the Shema. The original Shema from Deut 6:5 reads, "Love the LORD your God with all your heart, with all your soul, and with all your strength." But in Mark 12:30, Jesus expands it, saying, "Love the Lord your God with all your heart, with all your soul, with all your mind, and with all your strength." The addition of "mind" is striking and theologically significant. It wasn't a slip of memory or a casual rephrasing—it was divine reformation.

In doing this, Jesus was not violating the commandment, but fulfilling it with fuller intent. No one has the right to edit Scripture—unless they are God. And Jesus, the Word made flesh, has every right to bring greater clarity and completion to God's commands. In this, he affirms that true devotion includes cognitive engagement. Intellect is not optional in worship. Loving God includes thinking deeply, reasoning rightly, and knowing truly.

This directly echoes Mark Noll's lament. The reason there is so little evidence of an evangelical mind is because we have failed to love God with all of it. We have been compromised and distracted—discipled more by culture than by Christ. To love God with all your mind means more than intellectual assent or surface-level engagement, it calls for a Spirit-filled pursuit of truth, a sacred commitment to think Christianly in every arena of life.

Whether in business, science, politics, or the arts, it means bringing every thought captive to Christ. It's not merely about Bible knowledge but about forming a worldview saturated with Scripture and shaped by the Spirit. A renewed mind becomes the Spirit's instrument for discernment, cultural engagement, and kingdom transformation in a confused and collapsing world.

After Jesus' resurrection, Luke records that "He opened their minds to understand the Scriptures" (Luke 24:45). Jesus was not content with emotional belief—he trained thinking disciples. The recovered Christian mind is about thinking differently. It is about engaging truth and standing on it regardless of the outcome.

・・・・・・・・・・・・・・・・・・・・・・・・・・・・・・・・

A Spirit-empowered mind is not just informed—it is inflamed, alive with wisdom that can read the times and respond with courage.

・・・・・・・・・・・・・・・・・・・・・・・・・・・・・・・・

In 1 Chr 12:32, the sons of Issachar are described as "men who understood the times and knew what Israel should do." May their tribe increase. This ancient description could not be more relevant for the modern church. We live in a cultural fog where truth is questioned, identity is fluid, and convictions are optional. To understand the times today requires more than casual observation, it demands a Spirit-empowered mind shaped by biblical wisdom.

This is the high calling for every believer: to possess not just a redeemed heart but a renewed mind. The church's failure to cultivate this has rendered it largely silent, timid, and ineffective. But the Spirit invites us to think differently, to become people who discern rightly, reason courageously, and act faithfully.

This leads us into the next essential element of transformation: the Spirit's role in renewing the mind. Without his power, our thoughts are just good intentions. With his presence, our thinking becomes a weapon of light in a world of shadows.

THE SPIRIT'S ROLE IN MENTAL RENEWAL

This is where the Spirit Apex connects to the mind vertex in the Kingdom Triangle. The word "apex" is intentional. It is the highest and most prominent point of transformation. Without the Spirit, the mind remains tethered to human limitation, defaulting to fear, flesh, and faulty reasoning. But when the Spirit takes his rightful place at the apex, everything changes. Gordon Fee writes, "To have a renewed mind is equal to having the Spirit . . . a radically renewed mind, of a totally new way of viewing everything, brought about by the Holy Spirit."[15]

15. Fee, *Paul, the Spirit, and the People*, 95.

Christians Have Lost Their Minds!

This radical renewal is not subtle; it is a reorientation of perception, priorities, and purpose. It is seeing the world, others, and ourselves through the lens of heaven. Paul's call in Rom 12 is not a gentle suggestion—it is an imperative. "Be transformed by the renewing of your mind" is not optional for believers; it is a command. This transformation equips us to bring every thought captive to the obedience of Christ (2 Cor 10:5). Orthodoxy, right belief, leads to orthopraxy, right action. But wrong belief will never produce righteous behavior. Only a Spirit-empowered mind can resist the mental conformity of this age and walk in the truth that sets us free.

This is the battleground where the insidious ideologies of naturalism and postmodernity strike hardest. Their aim is to displace divine truth with self-directed autonomy and redefine reality on humanity's terms. It is only through the Spirit's renewal that the believer can stand against these demonic anti-God worldviews.

Consider Paul on Mars Hill in Acts 17. He stood before the intellectual elite of his day, the philosophers of Athens, and reasoned with them logically and persuasively. He walked them through their own categories and constructs, but when he arrived at the resurrection of the dead, a truth their worldview could not accommodate, they ended the conversation. That is the pattern of the world: it will tolerate Christian thought only to a point.

But it is not just apologetics or rhetoric that bears witness to a broken world; it is the humility, compassion, and unshakable conviction of those who live surrendered to truth. That is the Stockdale Christian, standing firm amidst the brutal reality of Babylon, empowered not by cleverness but by the Spirit of God.

One of the most beautiful depictions of discipleship is found in Luke 24: the extraordinary picture of the risen Jesus walking with two unsuspecting, discouraged disciples on the road to Emmaus. They were disillusioned, downcast, and grieving the apparent failure of their hopes. Like so many of us, they couldn't reconcile what they believed with what they had just experienced. They had all the facts, but not the framework. They had data, but no illumination. And then, Jesus shows up. Not with condemnation, but with presence. He comes alongside, not just to walk but to explain. He opens the Scriptures and begins to connect every passage, every shadow, every prophecy to himself. Imagine that, having the Author of Scripture interpret it for you. The mind is a terrible thing to waste, and Jesus refuses to let his disciples remain in confusion. He redeems their perspective, renews their minds, and restores their hope.

By the time they sat to eat, their hearts were burning, their despair had lifted, and their minds were electrified. They were transformed, not just emotionally uplifted but mentally awakened. This is the very essence of what it means to recover the Christian mind: not merely accumulating information, but experiencing illumination. Not just parsing verses, but encountering the living Word behind them. Their minds were renewed, not through clever arguments but through divine presence and revealed truth.

That moment wasn't just a history lesson; it was a Spirit-fueled mental awakening. And it is the model for us. We recover the Christian mind by walking with Jesus, letting the Spirit interpret the word, and allowing our minds to be set on fire by truth.

RECOVERING THE CHRISTIAN MIND: A STRATEGY

We've seen the depths of the problem, the depravity of the natural mind, the cultural drift, and the theological compromise. But now, we turn to practical renewal. This is where we clean house. Some of our mental furniture must go. Some beliefs must be evicted. And this is not a gentle rearranging of decor—it's a full demolition. Remodeling begins with a violent undoing of what no longer fits. That's painful. Especially when those old walls are made of beliefs we once championed, convictions we once preached, and assumptions we never thought to question.

But kingdom living requires kingdom thinking. The Spirit doesn't patch up old mental blueprints—he rewrites them. Just as Paul declared, "We destroy arguments and every lofty opinion raised against the knowledge of God" (2 Cor 10:5), we must submit our thought patterns to divine inspection. The Spirit doesn't want to rent space in our minds; he wants to tear down strongholds, evict squatters, and rebuild with holy fire.

This is the high cost of transformation. It's not theoretical—it's surgical. It is the painful collision of past and present, of falsehood and truth. But on the other side of demolition is freedom. And the first step toward recovery is not information—it's repentance. Let's begin there.

Before we step into renewal, we must confront the damage. Just as with any real renovation, the deeper you go, the more you discover: dry rot behind the walls, mold in the rafters, pests in the crawl spaces. Spiritually, it's the same. Some strongholds are hidden beneath theological wallpaper and emotional paint. We can't patch them. They must be torn out.

This is where the Spirit begins his work, not by gently dusting off the mind but by exposing its cracks. He shines the flashlight under the crawl space and asks, "Are you ready to address this?" These are painful revelations: flawed assumptions, half-truths, cultural compromises we once taught and defended. But now, we find ourselves in conflict with them because they no longer fit within a kingdom worldview. It's not just admitting we were wrong. It's surrendering what we once called right.

....

Recovering the mind is only the beginning. Truth must penetrate deeply to restore the soul, or knowledge will harden into arrogance instead of ripening into transformation.

....

Demolition is painful because the brokenness being exposed is not someone else's, it's ours. And so, before reconstruction begins, a spiritual inspection must take place. We must let the Holy Spirit point to every termite of naturalism, every rodent of postmodernity, every faulty beam of self-righteousness. If we skip this step, we build in vain.

Jesus asked in Luke 6:46, "Why do you call me Lord, Lord, and do not do what I say?" That's the question that cuts through the fog. Are we willing to tear down what he never built?

If so, the Spirit will not leave us in rubble. He provides a clear path forward. What follows are four Spirit-led steps that move us from demolition to renewal, from collapse to reconstruction.

1. Take Ownership of Your Condition

Begin by praying Ps 139:23–24:

> Search me, God, and know my heart;
> test me and know my concerns.
> See if there is any offensive way in me;
> lead me in the everlasting way.

Renewal starts here, with brutal honesty before God. Demolition is never pretty, but without it there can be no rebuilding. The Spirit shines his light into our hearts, exposing what we would rather keep hidden. That exposure is painful, but it is also merciful, for what is revealed can now be healed.

This is the Stockdale Paradox applied to the Christian mind: face the brutal facts without losing hope. Proverbs 1:7 reminds us, "The fear of the Lord is the beginning of knowledge," yet too often we've feared irrelevance more than God. Like the Laodiceans in Rev 3:17, we imagine ourselves rich in understanding but are actually poor, blind, and naked.

True reformation begins with repentance, with handing over the keys of the mind to the Spirit, our Master Contractor. Only then can the work of renewal begin.

2. Assess Your Beliefs

Many Christians can describe how they feel about God but struggle to explain why they believe. Yet everyone has a worldview, the lens through which they interpret life, even if few can articulate it clearly. That's why assessing your beliefs begins with holding your assumptions, attitudes, and interpretations up to the grid of Scripture.

Peter commands, "Always be ready to give a defense to anyone who asks you for a reason for the hope that is in you" (1 Pet 3:15). This is more than evangelism; it is apologetics of both the mind and heart. Like the Bereans in Acts 17:11, we are called to search the Scriptures daily, not just to confirm what we already believe but to correct where we have gone off course.

The Spirit leads this work with precision. Paul reminds us in 2 Cor 10:5 that strongholds must be torn down, not tolerated. That demolition can be painful because it touches the very frameworks on which we've built our thinking. Yet God is not reckless in this process. He is careful, surgical, and purposeful. His aim is not destruction but deliverance.

If your worldview cannot be explained biblically and lived out faithfully, it is not a worldview worth keeping. Renovation requires full exposure to the light of God's truth and full surrender to his authority.

3. Change Your Inputs

What fills your mind shapes your faith. Scripture reminds us, "Faith comes by hearing, and hearing by the word of Christ" (Rom 10:17). If we constantly consume the noise of culture, media, entertainment, and endless distraction, our thoughts will inevitably drift with it. But when we increase our intake of Scripture, sound teaching, and wise counsel, our minds are reshaped by truth.

Psalm 1 describes the blessed person as one who delights in God's law and meditates on it day and night. The psalmist echoes this throughout Psalm 119:

- "I have hidden your word in my heart that I might not sin against you" (verse 11).
- "Your word is a lamp to my feet and a light to my path" (verse 105).
- "The unfolding of your words gives light; it gives understanding to the simple" (verse 130).

God's word is not mere information—it is formation. It reshapes our thoughts, governs our desires, and anchors our lives in wisdom.

Sometimes this requires fasting, not only from food but from constant input. Stepping away from noise makes space for clarity. Paul offers a practical filter in Phil 4:8: whatever is true, honorable, just, pure, lovely, commendable—if anything is excellent or praiseworthy—think about these things. This is the input strategy of a sanctified mind: it doesn't just abstain from corruption; it fills itself with what is holy.

Change your inputs and you will change your instincts. What you feed your mind today becomes the faith you live tomorrow.

4. Invite the Spirit

Mental renewal is not a self-improvement project. You cannot think your way into transformation. The Spirit is not an accessory to clarity—he is the source of clarity. Without him, our minds remain clouded; with him, we see truth clearly.

Paul's prayer in Eph 1:17-18 should be ours: that the God of our Lord Jesus Christ may give you the Spirit of wisdom and revelation in the knowledge of him. The Spirit is our Counselor, Advocate, and Illuminator. He comes alongside to guide, correct, and strengthen, enabling us to think rightly and live courageously.

The disciples on the road to Emmaus had the facts, but it was the presence of Jesus and the illumination of the Spirit that made their hearts burn and their minds awaken. That is what the Spirit does—he doesn't just explain truth; he ignites it.

Invite him daily. Yield your thoughts to his inspection. Ask for his wisdom in your decisions. Welcome his conviction when you drift. Renewal doesn't happen by adding more content but by surrendering to his control. A Spirit-led mind is not just informed—it is aflame.

When we walk these four Spirit-led steps, the mind is no longer a cluttered attic of confusion but a sanctified instrument in the hands of God. Our thoughts align with heaven's truth. Our convictions hold steady against cultural currents. Our imagination is captured by his promises rather than by empty temptations.

But renewal is not optional—it is survival. Without clarity, we drift. Without discernment, we crash. Just like a ship without a compass, the Christian who neglects the mind is destined to run aground.

THE SS DOMINATOR WAS DOMINATED

In March of 1961, the Greek freighter *SS Dominator* ran aground off the rocky coast of Palos Verdes, California. An experienced captain with more than twenty years at sea was making his first voyage along the West Coast. That evening, a dense fog dropped over Rocky Point, shrouding everything in blindness.

The *Dominator*, carrying nine thousand tons of wheat and beef from Vancouver to Algeria, had no radar or modern navigation equipment. Slowing his 441-foot vessel to just eleven knots, the captain hoped to find the Port of Los Angeles to refuel. Instead, disoriented by the fog and without true bearings, he drove the freighter directly into the rocks.

The *Dominator* was dominated, shipwrecked, not by sabotage or storm but by lack of clarity. The tragedy was avoidable, but the consequences were permanent.

As Christ followers, we cannot afford to navigate the shallow waters of culture without insight, understanding, and wisdom. To drift without conviction is to risk shipwrecking our faith on the rocks of ignorance. Like the sons of Issachar, we must understand the times and know what to do, or we too will be destroyed for lack of knowledge.

Jesus has handed us the coordinates. The Spirit is our compass. The word is our map. It's time to reclaim our minds and renew our thinking—not as ghost towns of empty thoughts, but as a Spirit-empowered army of transformed minds.

BEYOND THE MIND—TOWARD WHOLENESS

And yet, for all the firepower of a renewed mind, transformation is not complete unless the whole person is engaged. The mind may be discerning and aligned, but the integrated life God intends requires more. It requires wholeness. It requires soul. But not any soul will do.

This is where the next leg of our journey leads. If the renewed mind is the engine, the restored soul is the fuel tank. When the mind is aligned but the soul is fragmented, weariness sets in. Busyness replaces intimacy. Hustle overtakes peace. We may know the truth but still feel hollow—that is the tragedy of the empty self.

In chapter 6, we move from cognition to integration, from sharp thought to deep presence. We will explore what it means to live as a Shalom Soul—a life marked by peace, purpose, and wholeness in an empty-self culture obsessed with image, performance, and distraction.

CHAPTER 6

Shalom Soul vs. the Empty Self

Our hearts are restless until they rest in You.

—Augustine, *Confessions*

In the wilderness, Israel walked with God by fire and cloud. They saw miracles, ate manna, and yet their affections drifted. Familiarity with the sacred bred contempt. The whisper of Eden—"Did God really say?"—echoed again. Likewise, the modern church has not been overtaken by external powers, but seduced by internal apathy. It has wandered from a gritty Stockdale resilience to a coddled Stockholm compromise. Chains are now called security, and captivity is dressed in relevance.

Laodicea was a church that thought it needed nothing, yet Christ was on the outside knocking. What causes a church to become so tepid and useless that even Jesus becomes nauseous? It is the loss of identity and the championing of the enemy we were called to resist. Cold water refreshes. Hot water heals. Lukewarm water does neither. It is not fit for its intended use. In mimicking the culture's temperature, the church forfeits its power. When relevance replaces reverence, and affirmation replaces transformation, we become spiritually lukewarm, comfortable, compromised, and ineffective.

Yet Jesus speaks these harsh words not in rejection but in sorrow and holy disappointment. He disciplines those he loves. His warning is not abandonment; it is an invitation to repentance. His parting words to all the churches in Revelation echo with urgency and hope: "Anyone who has an ear should listen to what the Spirit says to the churches."[1] The door is not locked. He is still knocking. But we must be willing to hear, to open, and to return.

· ·

The soul was never meant to live on borrowed fire. When reverence fades, the heart drifts into apathy, and a church that settles for comfort soon discovers it has nothing left to confront the world with.

· ·

We flatter Pharaoh. We trade our inheritance for instant gratification. We applaud expressive autonomy and call it freedom. But Admiral Stockdale's paradox remains: brutal reality must be faced, but never without hope. The church, however, has embraced the darkness without discernment and calls it progress. The diagnosis is anthropological as much as theological—we have forgotten what it means to be human.

ANATOMY OF THE EMPTY SELF—PASSIVE, PROGRAMMED, AND ADDICTED

I wasn't in the business of remodels; I built new homes. That's why the call caught me off guard. A woman I'd never met was nearly in tears on the other end of the line. She and her husband had just purchased a stunning Spanish-style estate nestled in the highlands of San Juan Capistrano. On the outside, the house was postcard-perfect: red tile roof, graceful archways, and a sweeping view across 6.5 acres with a distant ocean view. But they had unknowingly bought a biohazard.[2]

The home was rat-infested—unlivable. Their inspector had opened exploratory holes in the drywall, and the news wasn't just bad—it was catastrophic. The infestation wasn't superficial. It was systemic. That's when they called me.

I drove out to meet them, still unsure if I would take the job. I told them up front: I don't do remodels. But as I walked the property, I saw

---

1. Rev 1–3.
2. Johnson, *Renovation Project* contains the entire story of this project. I use it to parallel our personal renovation journey and the development of a Christian worldview.

desperation in their eyes. So I gave them three options: One, flip it as fast as possible and let someone else deal with the mess. Two, bulldoze the entire structure and rebuild from scratch. Or three, strip it to the studs, inspect every inch, and rebuild what could be salvaged. They chose option three.

The previous owner had tried to mask the stench with candles and cosmetics. But you can't air-freshen your way out of toxic infestation. It had to be gutted. Not because the furniture was out of date or the marble floors and the brass handrails weren't polished enough, but because it was structurally compromised. The rats had made a home in every part of that house: walls, vents, cabinets, and crevices. But it wasn't the feces that caused the deepest problem—it was the urine. The hidden filth had soaked into the structure itself.

Demo day confirmed the worst. The moment we peeled back the drywall, we were hit by a stench that no air freshener could hide. The rat urine had saturated the framing. It had corroded steel saddles and hold-downs, rusted bolts, and seeped into load-bearing beams. The bones of the house were diseased. No amount of surface cleaning would suffice. It needed total reconstruction—surgical demolition before redemption.

That's the anatomy of the empty self. It looks good on the outside, but inside, it's rotting. It's a carefully arranged soul with spiritual termites: addicted to distraction, allergic to depth, hollowed out by artificial stimulation. Like this San Juan house, many of us have learned to live with the stench. Just light another candle. Spray more Febreze. Call it the new normal.

Psychologist Philip Cushman exposes the "empty self" as a cultural construction: passive, lonely, anxious, and stripped of purpose.[3] It is the ideal consumer, addicted to distraction and allergic to depth. Our souls are shaped by algorithms, not cultivated by truth. James K. A. Smith reminds us we are not merely thinkers, but lovers. What we love shapes who we become.[4] And we love what entertains us.

The word "amuse" comes from the root "muse," meaning to think or ponder. Add the prefix *a*, and it becomes its opposite: not to think. Amusement, then, is the suspension of thought. It is the act of checking one's mind at the door for the sake of diversion. In many churches today, amusement has become the metric of engagement. We do not ask, "Did it shape me?" but "Did I enjoy it?"

3. Cushman, *Constructing the Self*, 312–35.
4. Smith, *You Are What You Love*.

We have become a church that requires entertainment. We treat worship like a concert, preaching like a TED Talk, and spiritual formation like content creation. But diversion is not discipleship. The more we are amused, the less we are formed. Entertainment, when unchecked, becomes a spiritual sedative, masking our emptiness rather than healing it. We are raising generations who have been amused into apathy.

A sedated soul cannot carry kingdom weight. Amusement may numb the ache, but only surrender brings healing. Until the church trades diversion for discipleship, it will keep producing spectators instead of saints.

This is the hallmark of the empty self. It cannot sit in silence. It cannot wrestle with mystery. It seeks distraction over depth, spectacle over substance. And in doing so, it becomes increasingly hollow, increasingly unrecognizable, even to itself.

Entertainment addiction is not neutral. Media directs our affections and dulls our discernment. We do not merely watch movies; they reprogram us. The rise of deism among Christian youth, the quoting of sitcoms over Scripture, the worship of relevance over reverence—these are not cultural quirks. They are soul-shaping forces.

Movies teach worldviews. Philosophy is embedded in the storylines. And as Orson Welles admitted, "I hate television. I hate it as much as peanuts. But I can't stop eating peanuts."[5] Entertainment has become a sedative.

Like peanuts, we keep consuming, even when we're no longer hungry, just to feel something. But instead of being nourished, we're numbed. Instead of transformation, we get distraction. We live in a time where Netflix bingeing is therapeutic and YouTube algorithms disciple more consistently than Sunday sermons.

The empty self is not simply a product of moral failure. It's a casualty of misdirected formation. Dick Staub warns that Christians have not only been poorly catechized, they've been reprogrammed by pop culture. He adds, "We have replaced the transformative gospel with a consumer-friendly

---

5. Welles, quoted in Postman, *Amusing Ourselves to Death*, 87.

version—one that doesn't confront but coddles, that entertains rather than equips, and that delivers comfort rather than calling."[6]

And it leaves us starving.

This is the paradox of the empty self: it is never full and always famished. It gorges on stimulus yet remains hollow. We scroll, consume, click, and refresh, but the ache doesn't go away. It deepens. Because what we crave is not more content—but connection. Not more dopamine—but meaning. Not more relevance—but reverence. The problem with living for the next happiness fix is that it's never enough. The empty self needs more and more, bigger and better. It's the spoiled anthem of a starving soul.

Until we name the emptiness, we cannot be filled. And until we admit the infestation, we will never be healed. There is a better way, but first, the house must be exposed. Then rebuilt.

FRAGMENTATION—THE COLLAPSE OF WHOLENESS

Before a structure can be restored, it must first be stripped. At the San Juan site, no amount of patching or staging could have saved that house from collapse. The damage ran too deep. We had to gut it to the studs, not out of punishment but for preservation. And this is what must happen in the human soul.

The empty self is not merely distracted—it is disintegrated. It is the rot beneath the paint. Truth has become subjective, and with that shift, the pillars that once supported a cohesive identity have crumbled. Gender is no longer rooted in biology but preference. Morality is a matter of opinion. Entitlement replaces responsibility, and feelings replace facts. Without metaphysical anchors, the self drifts in cultural winds.

When people no longer ask the big questions—Who am I? Why am I here? What is true?—they lose cohesion. And when cohesion vanishes, identity fractures. Stewart Goetz and Charles Taliaferro, in *A Brief History of the Soul*,[7] trace this to the philosophical rejection of the soul. The consequences are staggering. Without the soul, there is no enduring identity, only psychological snapshots. There is no essence, just evolving preferences.

And more critically, if there is no soul, there is nothing to survive death and the grave. The biblical vision of human worth, eternal life, and communion with God collapses into dust. In its place, we're told to look

---

6. Staub, *Culturally Savvy Christian*, 42.
7. Goetz and Taliaferro, *Brief History of the Soul*, 202–15.

inward and craft our own meaning—a meaning that cannot outlive mortality. We no longer believe there is a "self" to be formed—only impulses to be followed.

Into that vacuum rushes counterfeit transcendence; entertainment has become religion. It disciples with greater frequency, emotional engagement, and formative power than most churches. Algorithms now shape our stories more than Scripture. Fragmentation is the new normal.

Paul Vitz helps us see another layer: the psychological roots. He links fatherlessness to atheism and identity confusion. If God is Father, then to grow up without a father, or with a distorted one, is to experience a spiritual vacuum. In *Faith of the Fatherless*, Vitz provides striking illustrations. Friedrich Nietzsche, David Hume, and Jean-Paul Sartre all lost their fathers young. Vitz doesn't argue that every atheist lacks a father, but he observes a recurring pattern: absent or abusive fathers correlate with a deep rejection of God. And even where fathers were present, if they were cold, passive, or overly authoritarian, they often projected a distorted image of God.[8]

The result? Our narratives turn inward. God is removed from the equation. Our identities turn fluid, no longer shaped by divine imprint but by human impulse. Our souls turn hollow—orphans in search of origin.

This fragmentation isn't just philosophical or psychological; it's physiological. And, though we discussed this in the last chapter, it is not relegated to the mind. Dopamine is now our priest. This God-given neurotransmitter, meant to be a motivator toward life-giving behaviors, has been hijacked. It's now weaponized through binge cycles of food, fantasy, gambling, porn, gaming, and scrolling. Our culture has become addicted to what I refer to as "cultural ice cream"—pleasures that stimulate the senses but deaden the soul.

The problem isn't merely that we're tempted; it's that we've restructured our brains to crave temptation. The enemy knows this. He doesn't just bait with sin; he builds a system that keeps our dopamine levels unstable and hungry. The more we indulge, the more we need to indulge just to feel normal. We are not resisting the culture, we are consuming it, and calling it Christian.

This is the bait-and-switch of our age. We long for meaning, but settle for media. We seek shalom, but binge dopamine. The result is not simply a morally compromised church—it is a neurochemically compromised one.

---

8. Vitz, *Faith of the Fatherless*, 16–19.

A church that needs its entertainment fix, its emotional high, its sugar-coated spirituality. And we wonder why we are fragmented.

Sin is pleasurable—for a season. But it comes with a buried hook. Our enemy lures us out of the deep waters of God's love and into the frying pan of shame and addiction. And when the dopamine crash hits, he whispers that we are unworthy, unlovable, and unredeemable. The cycle repeats.

We must cut the circuit of false reward and rewire around the presence of God. The Holy Spirit is not just a comforter—he is the soul's Master Architect. He alone knows what you were made to crave. And it isn't cultural ice cream. It's living water.

Fragmentation doesn't have to be our fate. But until we confront our biochemical, emotional, and spiritual addiction—and surrender it to Christ—we will keep collapsing.

Wholeness begins with holy demolition. Only then can we rebuild a soul that can house the presence of God.

THE MYTH OF SELF-FULFILLMENT

The modern gospel has been baptized in self-help and packaged in motivational sound bites. In an age where self-actualization is the highest aim and emotional happiness is the ultimate virtue, we've been sold a lie: that fulfillment comes from fame, success, or the thoughtfully managed life. But reality keeps breaking through the illusion.

Few testimonies have captured this better than that of Matthew Perry. In his memoir *Friends, Lovers, and the Big Terrible Thing*, Perry reflected that fame did not resolve his inner battles—"I thought fame would fix everything. It didn't. It made everything worse."[9] Behind the sitcom laughter and public acclaim was a man locked in a brutal battle with addiction and despair. At the height of his success, he confessed to feeling isolated and hollow, a slave to the very pleasures the world promised would satisfy.

This emptiness is not limited to celebrities. It plays out in the culture's repeated mantras. Consider Veruca Salt from *Willy Wonka and the Chocolate Factory*. Her infamous demand, "I want it now!" is the egocentric soundtrack of a generation taught that desire justifies everything. She is the personification of a culture that refuses to wait, refuses to sacrifice, and demands that fulfillment arrive on command. Her shrill impatience echoes through our media, marketing, and even ministry.

9. Perry, *Friends*, 230.

Shalom Soul vs. the Empty Self

The cumulative effect is a catechism of immediacy, one that shapes not only buying habits but belief systems. What are TV ads really selling? They're not just selling products; they're selling you and me. The implicit message is that we are incomplete without this, inferior if we don't have that, and behind if our neighbor has one and we don't. It's a campaign of discontent—a perpetual feed-the-beast strategy to keep you striving, spending, and never satisfied.

This is the problem with living for happiness—it's a beast that is never satisfied. Happiness is a great servant but a treacherous master. When it is in control, its only enemy is—wait for it—boredom. We were never designed to live for happiness. That idea would have baffled the classical philosophers. For Aristotle, happiness (*eudaimonia*) was not about momentary pleasure but about living a virtuous life—a life of purpose, discipline, and moral excellence. In the biblical worldview, joy flows from obedience and purpose, not indulgence.

The self wasn't meant to be actualized; it was meant to be crucified. But the therapeutic gospel offers Jesus as a life coach, not a crucified King. We end up with disciples who crave affirmation but cannot handle sacrifice. The church becomes a boutique, not a battalion. And the soul is still starved.

This empty self is driven by distraction, addicted to affirmation, and allergic to discipline. It cannot handle denial. It fears silence. It flees responsibility. "The empty self," Moreland and Klaus Issler write, "is filled up with consumer goods, calories, experiences, [and] lacks personal conviction and worth.... It embodies the absences as a chronic, undifferentiated emotional hunger."[10] It is an anti-soul, a structure built to collapse.

This is not a peripheral issue. The empty self is the soul-shaped casualty of postmodern fragmentation and consumeristic discipleship. It is what the church becomes when we choose relevance over repentance, comfort over formation, and happiness over holiness. It is also the default self of Western culture.

Which means that unless we intentionally renovate the soul, unless we demolish the scaffolding of the empty self and rebuild with biblical patterns of transformation, we will not survive the coming pressures. Dick Staub's reference to Christianity Lite is so very fitting. It may taste great for a while, but it will never satisfy . . . like ever.

---

10. Moreland and Issler, *Lost Virtue of Happiness*, 26.

BLUEPRINT FOR RENOVATION

The San Juan project is a parable of the soul.

We live in a world that decorates dysfunction, that lights scented candles over corruption and pretends everything is fine. We spray air freshener and hang welcome signs in foyers filled with moral rot. But God is not into pretending. He doesn't put a clothespin on his nose and smile politely at the decay. He is not into whitewashing tombs or painting over filth. He deals in light, truth, and reality. He sees through the drywall of denial and goes straight to the studs.

And that is why God is never interested in option #1 or option #2: he doesn't sell us off as hopeless, and he doesn't bulldoze what bears his image. He only ever chooses option #3: surgical, systematic, redemptive restoration. Because he knows what we could become if we give him full access to begin the demo, address the infestation, and build us back into a house of glory.

And the Holy Spirit is our divine contractor. He does not impose. He waits for permission. But once invited in, he begins pulling drywall, opening windows, and purging the infestation. His work is precise. Holy. Hopeful.

And it all begins with truth. Not cosmetic patchwork. Not denial. Not distraction. But full exposure. The Spirit enters the house. He brings light into forgotten places. He removes the infestation. He rebuilds not around our preferences, but around his presence.

Dallas Willard describes the soul as the integration of all dimensions of human life: thoughts, feelings, choices, body, social context, and spirit, around God.[11] When those areas are fragmented or governed by the flesh, the soul becomes disordered. Renovation brings those parts back into alignment through

- self-denial and cross-bearing (Luke 9:23),
- spiritual disciplines that train desires (1 Tim. 4:7),
- apprenticeship to Jesus, not just belief in Jesus (Matt 9:9).

Anyone entering into a substantial remodel understands it all begins with demo. The old must be stripped out: drywall removed, rot exposed, infestation addressed. It's not optional. It's foundational. A kitchen can't be

---

11. Willard, *Renovation of the Heart*, 37–40.

restored if the mold behind the cabinets remains. No builder would install fresh floors over a urine-saturated substructure.

Likewise, the Spirit won't redecorate a soul built on spiritual decay. He won't paint over bitterness, resentment, or pride. He removes. He purges. Then he rebuilds.

• •

The difference between believing disciples and bold witnesses is the fire of the Spirit. Without him, the soul drifts into emptiness; with him, it flourishes in shalom.

• •

The blueprint for the Shalom Soul begins with hard truth. With full exposure. With a spiritual demo that is disruptive, humbling, and essential. We must reject the myth that change happens automatically. Transformation is intentional. And soul work, like demo, is slow, hidden, painful, and essential.

THE SHALOM SOUL—A SACRED RESTORATION

Shalom is not peace as the world gives—it is total integration, wholeness, purpose, and harmony. The Shalom Soul is aligned with God and others. It is healed, not hyped. Filled, not fabricated. Jesus said, "Peace I give you . . . not as the world gives" (John 14:27). This is the echo of Eden and the whisper of the kingdom.

Dallas Willard reminded us, "The human soul is not made to run on empty. It is made to be at home in God."[12] The Shalom Soul is not anxious, but anchored. Not drifting, but directed. It reflects the image it was made in.

This is the soul that can transform culture because it is no longer formed by it. It can suffer without breaking, serve without applause, and shine without self-promotion. The Shalom Soul is Christ's signature in the life of the believer. It is the wholeness we were made for.

If the Spirit ignites our power, the soul becomes the place where that fire is formed into character. The soul is the vessel God uses to carry his presence with durability. It is the center of gravity for all that makes us

---

12. Paraphrased from themes in Willard, *Renovation of the Heart*, ch. 2.

human: our thoughts, emotions, desires, and relationships, bound together in spiritual coherence. But without the Spirit, the soul lacks oxygen. It may long for wholeness but lacks the wind to shape it.

My former professor at Fuller Seminary, Ray Anderson, describes the human person as one who exists in relation to God and others, made in the *imago Dei*, reflecting the relational and purposeful nature of the Triune God. He writes, "Human beings are not simply biological entities with spiritual capacity; they are spiritual beings whose humanity is defined by their relation to God, others, and the world."[13] But we have forgotten who we are. The church's silence on soul formation has created a vacuum, and the culture has filled it with digital illusions, therapeutic deconstruction, and hyper-individualism.

The result? A spiritual crisis of identity. We don't know who we are, so we try on roles—consumer, influencer, victim, performer—while the soul underneath remains unformed. Our insides no longer match our outsides.

The solution is not found in retreating from the world, but in re-centering on God's original design for wholeness by allowing the Spirit to restore the soul from the inside out. Renovating the soul is not a human effort of self-help. It is a divine work of grace-fueled rehumanization, coordinated by the very Spirit we welcomed in the upper room.

Without the Spirit, the disciplines become dry. But with him, solitude becomes communion. Confession becomes cleansing. Silence becomes revelation. The renovation of the soul, rightly ordered, is the Spirit's way of forming fire into fidelity, of turning holy desire into daily resilience.

We are broken by sinful choices and an enemy whose goal is to separate us from our true identity in Christ. We cannot renovate ourselves. This is not a DIY project to fix ourselves. We need power from on high, just like my construction site needed power for all of the tools and equipment necessary to take on this project.

To renovate the soul is to be reshaped in the image of Christ from the inside out. This is slow work, spiritual carpentry, divine architecture. It is what Dallas Willard called "the renovation of the heart,"[14] where the fragmentation of the self is replaced by the wholeness of shalom. In this process, the emotional, relational, intellectual, and volitional parts of our lives are reintegrated under the lordship of Christ.

---

13. Anderson, *On Being Human*, 43.
14. Willard, *Renovation of the Heart*, 37–40.

The empty self, addicted to consumption, novelty, and escape, cannot survive cultural pressure. But the renovated soul can carry kingdom weight. It is deeply rooted, internally ordered, and capable of manifesting both compassion and conviction. When the soul is strong, the disciple is unshakable. And in an age of anxiety, spiritual superficiality, and endless stimulation, a deep soul is a prophetic protest.

Renovation is both resistance and renewal. It is how the kingdom is embodied, not in polished performances but in cross-bearing, truth-embracing, Spirit-formed people who embody the presence of Christ in a fractured world.

To rebuild the soul is to remember our origin. And to remember our origin is to reclaim our destiny. The soul matters. Because the human being, fully alive in Christ, is the enemy's greatest threat.

THE STOCKDALE ANTIDOTE: FROM FRAMEWORK TO FIRE

We have now journeyed through the three vertices of the Kingdom Triangle: Spirit, mind, and soul. Each piece, vital on its own, forms a sacred geometry that cannot fully function without the others. But what we've seen thus far are blueprints without power tools, puzzle pieces not yet interlocked, forms without fire.

We've examined the collapse of the empty self, the fragmentation of modern identity, and the spiritual architecture of wholeness. Yet we cannot will our way into renovation. And we cannot simply admire the triangle from afar. It must be activated.

This is the crucial turning point . . . the ignition. Without power from on high, the triangle remains theory. Without the Holy Spirit's infusion, our call to transformation is just another self-help endeavor. That is not what this book is about. It is not a finger-pointing manifesto or a call to try harder. It is an altar call for the Spirit to come and do what only he can do.

The Spirit is not an accessory to discipleship; he is its engine. Only he can connect the dots, empower the practice, and infuse the structure with supernatural strength. My heart, in writing this, is not simply that readers learn more, it is that they personally encounter the living God. That you, reader, would know there is more—much more—and that the Holy Spirit longs to fill your soul with the very power that raised Jesus from the dead.

This is also where the paradox becomes a path. The Stockdale Paradox, which teaches us to face brutal reality without losing hope, is not just a philosophical concept, it's a discipleship strategy. The Spirit-filled life is the only way we can both confront the cultural crisis with clarity and carry kingdom courage with integrity. We are not abandoning the paradox; we are energizing it.

The bifurcated road, the split path, becomes one where brutal facts and bold faith walk hand in hand. Where honesty meets hope. Where we stare into the collapse and declare that Christ still reigns.

So as we now prepare to step into the next chapter: "Power Protocol," may your mind be open. May your soul be surrendered. And may your spirit be ignited. The triangle is not just a model to admire. It is a kingdom algorithm to be lived. And the Spirit is ready to light the fuse.

CHAPTER 7

Power Protocol

The Spirit-filled life is not a deluxe edition of Christianity. It is part and parcel of the total plan of God for His people.

—A. W. TOZER, *KEYS TO THE DEEPER LIFE*

WHAT DO WE NEED to do to restore the Spirit's power and energize the triangle?

We can only restore the Spirit's power in our lives when we reside in the same power-source that Jesus lived with.

Let me explain it with a construction visual.

Shortly after the 6.7 Northridge earthquake in 1994, like so many other contractors, I found myself buried in work. I was a finish carpenter at the time. On one particular day, I was building and installing a fireplace mantel in the main living room. I set up my workbench directly in front of the mantel and then positioned my chop saw and portable table saw, arranged the air compressor, and plugged in my battery charger and, of course, my radio.

The last thing I grabbed was my heavy hundred-foot yellow power cord, which I ran into the garage to reach the only live outlet. Once connected, I made my way back to my setup and reached for the power strip. It was seven in the morning and quiet. I plugged the power cord into the power strip. But nothing happened.

The chop saw didn't work as I pressed the switch several times. Not a hum from the compressor. Not even a whisper of static from the radio.

Then I realized that I had not flipped the switch on my power strip. None of these tools would do anything without power. They were ready. They were all plugged in. I was ready. But without power, everything sat in silence—useless. Power from the live outlet in the garage was connected to my power strip. The power was so close; it was right there. I reached over and flipped the breaker. The light on the strip lit up red, the compressor hummed to life, and my radio begin playing an old Petra song: "Mine Field" (love that song).

Power tools without power are just expensive paperweights. That's when Phil 4:13 came to life for me: "I am able to do all things through Him who strengthens me." And, conversely, nothing without him. That strength is the Spirit's power. It's what activates the gifts, what enables the tools, what gets the job done.

That red light on the power strip became a metaphor: until it glows, I have no chance of fulfilling the job I've been called to do. I had the tools, the skills, the materials, and even the motivation—but I was still grounded. It wasn't until the current began to flow that everything in my hands came to life.

That's the Spirit's role in the believer's life. We can have doctrine, discipline, and desire, but without the Spirit, we're on standby.

We are built for power. We are wired for divine enablement. And just like those tools on the job site, we are ineffective until the switch is flipped and the Spirit flows. This isn't about potential; it's about power. Jesus made it clear: don't do anything until you receive it.

• •

A powerless church is not a neutral church—it is a defeated one. Until the breaker is flipped and the current flows, our theology remains theory and our mission remains dormant. The Spirit alone turns potential into power.

• •

The Holy Spirit is the kingdom's utility company, and until the Spirit's power flows, our lives are decorative but unproductive. Jesus told his disciples not to move until they received power from on high. He wasn't just offering a bonus feature; he was declaring the ignition sequence. Without the Spirit, our tools are silent. Our design is dormant. The lights stay off.

So we begin this chapter the way any wise builder would: by making the connection. The cord is plugged in. The wiring is sound. But now we must flip the switch.

A BIBLICAL JOURNEY OF EMPOWERMENT THROUGH THE OLD TESTAMENT

Before we move forward in understanding how the Holy Spirit empowers the church today, we must first look back. The Spirit didn't first show up at Pentecost. He's been present and active from the opening moments of creation, hovering over the waters in Gen 1. He empowered judges to deliver, prophets to speak, and kings to reign. He gave strength to warriors, wisdom to rulers, and revelation to visionaries.

But here's the key: under the old covenant, the Spirit's empowerment was selective, situational, and sovereign. He came upon individuals for specific purposes and moments—but even then, his power was unmistakable. The Spirit was not absent—he was foreshadowing a greater outpouring yet to come.

This section offers a biblical survey of those Old Testament figures who were empowered by the Spirit to accomplish divine tasks. Their stories are not just ancient history; they are breadcrumbs that lead us to the fullness of the Spirit available in Christ. They are previews of what was to become normative in the new covenant.

Let's take a brief survey of those who were empowered by the Spirit and see how God's presence showed up in their stories.

Take Joseph, for example. When Pharaoh looked at him, he didn't just see a wise administrator—he saw something supernatural at work. "Can we find anyone like this, a man who has God's Spirit in him?" (Gen 41:38). Joseph's insight in interpreting dreams and strategizing for famine wasn't just human brilliance—it was Spirit-born wisdom.

Moses, overwhelmed with the burden of leading the people, discovered that the Spirit could be shared. God told him, "I will take some of the Spirit who is on you and put the Spirit on them. They will help you bear the burden of the people" (Num 11:17). Leadership wasn't meant to be carried alone—the Spirit empowered a team.

Joshua, Moses' successor, was described as a man "who has the Spirit in him" (Num 27:18). His courage to step into the land of promise flowed not from personality, but from divine presence.

The judges of Israel experienced this power in dramatic ways. Othniel judged Israel when "the Spirit of the LORD came on him" (Judg 3:10). Gideon, timid and unsure, suddenly blew a trumpet of courage when "the Spirit of the LORD enveloped" him (Judg 6:34). Jephthah, the outcast warrior, was emboldened when "the Spirit of the LORD came on" him (Judg 11:29). And Samson, known for raw strength, found his feats possible only when "the Spirit of the LORD came powerfully on him" (Judg 14:6).

The prophets, too, bore witness. Isaiah declared, "The Spirit of the Lord GOD is on me, because the LORD has anointed me to bring good news to the poor" (Isa 61:1). Ezekiel was literally lifted to his feet by the Spirit's presence (Ezek 2:2) and later carried into a valley of dry bones where the Spirit would breathe life into death (Ezek 37:1).

Elijah called down fire from heaven and ran ahead of a chariot by "the power of the LORD" (1 Kgs 18:38, 46). His successor, Elisha, pleaded, "Please, let me inherit two shares of your spirit" (2 Kgs 2:9)—and received it. Zechariah, speaking to Zerubbabel, summed it up with a timeless word: "Not by strength or by might, but by My Spirit, says the LORD of Armies" (Zech 4:6).

What's remarkable about all of these stories is the unique way God met each person. There was no formula. No single outward manifestation. No repeatable sign that could box in the work of the Spirit. What we see instead is the supernatural breaking into the natural—divine power manifesting for divine purposes. Each person was empowered for a particular moment, assignment, or crisis: wisdom for administration, strength for battle, clarity for prophecy, courage for leadership, vision for direction.

The Spirit showed up not as a background theology but as a disruptive force of divine intent. These moments were not everyday occurrences; they were strategic God-moments, where heaven broke into human experience. They were the kingdom on display, not fully come but undeniably near.

These Old Testament glimpses were never meant to remain isolated. They pointed forward to something more—the age Jesus inaugurated when he brought the kingdom with him and left the Spirit to carry it forward through us.

A SPECIAL NOTE ON DAVID'S ANOINTING

Among all those empowered in the Old Testament, David's experience with the Holy Spirit holds a special place. His anointing by the prophet Samuel marked a decisive moment—not just for his kingship, but for the trajectory of Spirit empowerment. First Samuel 16:13 records, "So Samuel took the horn of oil and anointed him in the presence of his brothers, and the Spirit of the LORD came powerfully on David from that day forward." Unlike many others for whom the Spirit came temporarily and for a specific task, the Scripture emphasizes permanence in David's empowerment. It was not a passing visitation—it was a lifelong companionship.

This is also what makes David's cry in Ps 51 so poignant: "Do not take Your Holy Spirit from me." He had tasted life in the Spirit and could not bear the thought of divine withdrawal. David's anointing wasn't just about leading battles or writing songs; it was about intimacy with God and being a man after his own heart. His example foreshadows what would later become available to all believers in Christ: a continual, indwelling presence of the Holy Spirit.

AND THEN THERE WAS BEZALEL

His name doesn't usually make the Sunday school top ten list. He wasn't a prophet calling down fire, or a judge rallying armies, or a king ruling a nation. He was a craftsman—an artisan tucked into the shadows of Exodus. But when God set out to design his dwelling place among his people, he didn't call for another Moses or another Joshua. He called Bezalel.

Scripture records God's words with unusual clarity: "I have filled him with God's Spirit, with wisdom, understanding, and ability in every craft" (Exod 31:3). Pause on that for a moment. The same Spirit who thundered at Sinai, who parted seas and shook mountains, now rested upon a man holding chisels, hammers, and weaving tools.

Bezalel wasn't asked to deliver Israel in battle or confront Pharaoh in the courts. His calling was to carve wood, shape gold, embroider fabric, and craft furniture that would become the very meeting place between heaven and earth. The Spirit didn't make him less of an artisan—the Spirit made him the fullest version of one. His creativity became consecrated. His skill became supernatural. His craft became an act of worship.

Imagine him in his workshop, the smell of fresh-cut acacia wood in the air, hands steady as he measured and shaped the ark of the covenant. This was no ordinary project. Every cut, every polish, every thread carried eternal weight. The Spirit wasn't just inspiring him in flashes—it was filling him with wisdom, understanding, and ability.

STOCKDALE PARADOX CHRISTIANITY

*What the world dismisses as ordinary,
the Spirit redefines as extraordinary.*

And here's the beauty of Bezalel's story: it dismantles the lie that only preachers, prophets, and missionaries qualify for Spirit-filled living. God poured out his Spirit on a blue-collar craftsman so that his presence could dwell among his people. That means the Spirit can anoint the teacher in the classroom, the nurse in the hospital, the engineer at the drafting table, the mother raising her children, the mechanic with grease on his hands, and the artist painting late into the night. Wherever God's people work, his Spirit longs to empower.

If God filled Bezalel with his Spirit to carve wood and set gemstones, he will gladly fill you for the calling he has placed on your life. And, how do I know that? Jesus himself assured us, "If you then, who are evil, know how to give good gifts to your children, how much more will the heavenly Father give the Holy Spirit to those who ask Him?" (Luke 11:13). The invitation is open. The same Spirit who turned a craftsman into a vessel of divine creativity is ready to breathe on your gifts, your vocation, your calling.

Bezalel's story builds into this crescendo: you don't have to be Moses to matter. You don't have to stand on a platform to be powerful. You don't have to hold a title to be anointed. The Spirit of God delights in filling everyday people with extraordinary power so that in every workshop, every kitchen, every office, and every field, heaven's creativity touches earth through the hands of those who believe.

And if the Spirit could fill a craftsman to carve wood and shape gold, how much more does he long to fill the Son of Man himself—the One who came not just to redeem us but to model what Spirit-filled humanity looks like? Bezalel points us forward to the ultimate example of Spirit-empowered life: Jesus.

JESUS: OUR EXAMPLE TO FOLLOW

Jesus is not only our God to worship—he is our model, our example to follow and emulate. But think about it, if Jesus, being God, did all that he did simply because he was God, we've got a problem. Who can follow that?

How could he possibly be our example? He's infinite—the rest of us, not so much. So when Jesus invites us to follow him, there must be something we're missing.

That "something" is what theologians call *kenosis*—the self-emptying described in Phil 2. Jesus did not stop being divine, but he chose not to rely on his divine attributes independently. Instead, he lived as a man fully dependent on the Spirit. He was conceived by the Spirit (Luke 1:35), anointed by the Spirit at his baptism (Luke 3:22), led by the Spirit into the wilderness (Luke 4:1), and returned in the power of the Spirit to begin his ministry (Luke 4:14). When he taught, healed, and cast out demons, he did so in Spirit-empowered humanity.

This changes everything. It means that Jesus is not only the God we worship but the pattern we can follow. He shows us what life looks like when fully surrendered to and filled with the Spirit. His miracles demonstrate divine compassion, yes, but they also reveal what a human life can look like when animated by the Spirit of God.

We face a sobering reality. Much of modern Christianity has learned to run on education, programs, and personal effort, while treating the miraculous as rare and unusual. We pray more often for medicine to work than for God to move. We instinctively reach for human solutions first. It's as if we live in a polite naturalism—acknowledging the Spirit in theory but rarely expecting him to act in power. Yet for Jesus, the supernatural was normal. The kingdom of God was not a metaphor or an abstract idea—it was a reality that broke into everyday life. His miracles weren't staged performances to impress; they were signs of the kingdom advancing.

To follow Jesus, then, requires more than affirming his divinity. It means embracing his humanity as our Spirit-empowered pattern. If he did everything simply because he was divine, we could only worship him from a distance, we could never imitate him. But instead, he chose to live in dependence on the Spirit, setting aside the independent use of his divine privilege to show us what Spirit-filled humanity looks like. That changes everything. It means we can follow him—not by straining in self-effort, but by relying on the same Spirit who empowered him.

This is the restoration we need. The Spirit was never intended to be a jump-start for the first-century church and then retired into history. He remains the power source for every generation. The first believers understood this instinctively: they waited, they prayed, and they refused to move until power fell. And when it did, everything changed—boldness erupted, miracles multiplied, and lives were transformed.

If Jesus himself waited for power before launching his mission, what makes us think we can fulfill ours without it?

A UNIFIED WITNESS... DIVERSE MANIFESTATIONS

History also gives us countless witnesses to the Spirit's empowerment: ordinary men and women whose lives became extraordinary when touched by divine fire.

Charles Finney, once a sharp lawyer more comfortable in a courtroom than a pulpit, found himself undone by the Spirit's presence. He described waves of liquid love coursing through him, an encounter that logic could not explain but that launched him into revival preaching and social reform. His ministry wasn't born from a degree, but from a visitation.[1]

Smith Wigglesworth began as a humble plumber in Yorkshire. Illiterate until his wife taught him the Bible, his life turned upside down when the Spirit baptized him in fire at age forty-eight. From that moment, he became known as the "Apostle of Faith," boldly praying for the sick and watching God confirm his word with miracles around the world.[2]

Jackie Pullinger was just twenty-two when she boarded a ship headed east with little more than faith in her pocket. Landing in Hong Kong's infamous Walled City, she worked among addicts, gang members, and the broken. But everything shifted when she and those she served received the baptism of the Spirit. Hardened men found deliverance, heroin addicts were freed without withdrawal, and the darkest slums became places of light.[3]

Jack Deere, once a staunch Reformed theologian, built his life on airtight doctrine. But when confronted with undeniable healings and prophetic words, he faced a decision: cling to theology or yield to the Spirit. He chose surrender, and his ministry became a testimony to both biblical integrity and supernatural vitality.[4]

John Wimber's journey began in music halls, not churches. A former rock musician turned pastor, he famously asked, "When do we get to do the

---

1. Finney, *Memoirs*, 20–21.
2. Frodsham, *Smith Wigglesworth*, 34–36.
3. Pullinger and Quicke, *Chasing the Dragon*, 33–35, 77–80.
4. Deere, *Surprised by the Power*, 17–44.

stuff?"—healing the sick, casting out demons, and living like the book of Acts. His discovery that "everybody gets to play" became a rallying cry for everyday believers stepping into Spirit ministry.[5]

Brother André never held a pulpit or penned a book. He served as a humble lay brother in Montreal, tending gardens and opening doors. Yet his simple prayers brought thousands to healing, so much so that the chapel walls filled with discarded crutches. His quiet availability proved that intimacy with the Spirit is greater than any title.[6]

David Brainerd, frail and dying of tuberculosis, could have withdrawn into self-pity. Instead, he poured himself out in prayer and preaching to indigenous tribes. His tears in the snow melted the ground around him as he interceded, and his short life sparked awakening beyond what health or talent alone could achieve.[7]

From the ashes of trauma and the confines of tradition, Joyce Meyer experienced the liberating power of the Holy Spirit. His presence brought peace where there had been turmoil and courage where fear once ruled. What began as a story of survival became a worldwide ministry of restoration, as she now leads others into the same freedom she found in him.[8]

Luis Palau, the Argentinian evangelist often called the "Latin Billy Graham," rose from obscurity and poverty into a worldwide platform. Spirit-filled boldness marked his preaching as crowds encountered both truth and power. He carried fire across continents, bridging Evangelicals and charismatics with the Spirit's joy and clarity.[9]

The Spirit does not standardize his work. Finney's fire looked nothing like Pullinger's courage. Wigglesworth's miracles were different from Brother André's quiet trust. Brainerd's intercession did not mirror Meyer's healing words.

Their manifestations were as diverse as their callings—some healed, others taught, others wept, and others crafted. But all carried evidence of divine empowerment.

---

5. Wimber and Springer, *Power Evangelism*, 15–18.
6. Ranaghan, *Brother André*, 45–47, 62–65.
7. Brainerd, *Life and Diary*, 232–34.
8. Meyer, *Beauty for Ashes*, 13–20, 45–50.
9. Palau, *Life on Fire*, 25–30, 85–90.

The Spirit does not erase your identity—he ignites it. Ordinary gifts become kingdom weapons, everyday work becomes eternal worship, and what once seemed common carries the weight of divine presence.

FINAL OBSERVATION

So here's the challenge: What about you? Perhaps you already sense the Lord has a calling on your life. You feel the tug of divine purpose—you know you were made for more. But here's the truth: your current occupation may be your anointed starting point. Don't despise it. Don't overlook the sacred potential of where you are right now. Allow the Spirit to use your job, your skill, your position as the proving ground of kingdom impact. Be faithful where you are. Don't minimize your talents or craft; what you see as ordinary, God may see as strategic. When surrendered to the Spirit, your work can become a ministry.

Think back over the stories we've traced: from Joseph's wisdom to Bezalel's artistry, from David's courage to Isaiah's prophecy, from Finney's fire to Pullinger's compassion. The diversity is breathtaking. The Spirit never repeated himself in a formulaic way. Instead, he empowered each person uniquely, according to their calling and the need of the moment.

And that is precisely the point. The Spirit delights in diversity. He equips the body of Christ with a kaleidoscope of gifts, talents, and empowerments so that no one can claim to have the single template for Spirit-filled life. This variety itself becomes the argument against narrowing the evidence of Spirit baptism down to one gift.

Which brings us to an important clarification. While tongues may accompany Spirit baptism, it is not the exclusive evidence. The idea that speaking in tongues is the sole sign of Holy Spirit baptism cannot bear the weight of biblical testimony or Spirit history.

For some, this empowerment did include tongues; for others, it appeared in prophecy, boldness, wisdom, healing, or miraculous courage—or craftsmanship. The point is not uniformity but variety. As Pentecostal theologian Craig Keener observes, "Luke emphasizes diversity in the Spirit's manifestations to highlight God's freedom and creativity."[10]

For Luke, tongues are not random or meaningless utterances. As Keener explains, they portray "Spirit-inspired speech, a fulfillment of the eschatological promise of the prophetic Spirit" (Acts 2:17–18).[11] He emphasizes that this gift functions as a theological sign of empowerment for the church's cross-cultural mission (Acts 1:8). Luke also makes it clear that the hearers in Jerusalem understood enough to recognize that the disciples were praising God (Acts 2:11).[12] Tongues, then, are not mere ecstatic sounds but a prophetic symbol of God's global intention. Keener notes, "What better symbol of this cross-cultural empowerment for mission could have been available than the phenomenon of tongues, which he understands as inspired speech in languages the speakers had not learned?"[13]

Thus, tongues are rightly viewed as a sign of prophetic empowerment for witness, but not the only sign. As Keener points out, the doctrine of tongues as the singular "initial evidence" of Spirit baptism is relatively recent, arising mostly in the early twentieth-century Pentecostal movement, with some antecedents in Edward Irving's Catholic Apostolic Church of the 1830s.[14] While rooted in genuine observation of Luke's narrative, it was foreign to many earlier interpreters precisely because it was so different from their own experience.

In other words, tongues matter—but they are part of a larger mosaic of Spirit empowerment. The true evidence of the Spirit's filling is not narrowed to one manifestation but found in the church's bold, Spirit-driven alignment with God's mission. The real question isn't "Did you speak in tongues?" It's "Have you been filled with power from on high for the assignment God has given you?"

And that brings us to the next step. If the Spirit's filling is about empowerment for mission, then how do we posture ourselves to receive and live in that power? What does ignition look like for us today?

---

10. Keener, *Gift and Giver*, 53.
11. Keener, *Acts*, 2:806.
12. Keener, *Acts*, 2:822.
13. Keener, *Acts*, 2:823.
14. Keener, *Acts*, 2:826–27.

Stockdale Paradox Christianity

THE LAUNCH SEQUENCE: POWER PROTOCOL

We are standing at T-minus six. The countdown has begun. The Spirit Apex has been explored, the triangle is aligned, and ignition is next. When this Kingdom Triangle is energized by the Holy Spirit, power flows, and everything changes.

If this feels foreign to you, if your background, church tradition, or personal comfort zone has shaped your expectations of how God works, you may be carrying silent hesitation. Many are perhaps worried that they are going to burst out in tongues, have to raise their hands, or start going door to door witnessing. The fear of the unknown, and of losing control, is paralyzing. But the Spirit doesn't come to override your personality or make you into someone you're not. He comes gently, personally, and purposefully to make you the best version of the person he created you to be.

In Acts 2, everything changed. The Spirit was no longer visiting the few; he was indwelling the many. This was not hype; it was heaven taking residence.

Are you ready to step into a dimension where peace surpasses understanding, joy overflows without explanation, and talents are supernaturally activated for kingdom purpose? Are you ready for your mind to be renewed and your soul to be made whole?

Then it's time to stop merely attending church or performing your vocation in your own strength. It's time to let the divine invade your everyday life. This isn't emotionalism. It's not fanaticism. It's not going to make you weird or unrecognizable. It's going to make you fully alive. This is the fulfillment of what God has always intended for you.

It's about his kingdom advancing through your Spirit-empowered giftedness. This is the monumental shift from a capitulating Stockholm Syndrome Christian to a Stockdale Paradox gate-crashing Christian. Are you ready to proceed?

If you are ready, here is the countdown—six steps that move us from waiting to walking in Spirit-empowered life.

Countdown to Power

Stop Everything—Stop the busyness. Turn off the religious autopilot. Shut down the routines you've been leaning on, and create sacred space. The disciples had work to do, but Jesus told them not to start until the power came. Luke 24:49 says, "But stay in the city until you are empowered from on high."

This was not optional. It was the *only* way forward for effective kingdom living. Jesus himself did not begin ministry until he was "clothed with power" after his baptism and the Spirit's descent (Luke 3:21–22; 4:1, 14). You've got to stop what you're doing and how you have been "doing" Christianity. Find a quiet place and then . . .

Wait—Don't wait passively, but prayerfully. Waiting doesn't mean doing nothing, it means posturing your heart in expectancy. Acts 1:14 tells us the early believers were "continually united in prayer." Waiting means refusing to rush what only God can do in his time. "Blessed are those who hunger and thirst for righteousness" (Matt 5:6). Power doesn't come to the apathetic. It comes to the desperate. This is the heartbeat behind the early church waiting in the upper room—not passive waiting, but active longing. Quiet your mind in his presence, as Ps 46:10 says: be still and know that he is God.

Surrender—Yield your expectations, fears, and conditions. This is not about striving; it's about trust. As Jack Deere said, "I don't care what this does to my theology. I want everything You have for me."[15] True surrender opens the door for the Spirit to fill all the spaces we've previously kept closed.

Power cannot fill what pride and self-reliance occupy. Charles Finney felt like a wave of liquid love was poured through his body as he yielded fully to God.[16]

Ask in Faith—Ask with childlike faith and a humble heart. Jesus said in Luke 11:13, "How much more will the heavenly Father give the Holy Spirit to those who ask Him?" You don't have to beg. You don't have to bargain. The Father delights to give his Spirit to his children. Look at that phrase once again, "How much more . . ." There is no hoping or wishing the Father will connect the triangle. Ask and you shall receive!

Receive—This is not earned; it's received. Ephesians 5:18 simply commands, "Be filled with the Spirit." That's present tense and passive voice—meaning it's ongoing, and God does the filling. Open your heart. Breathe in grace. Welcome the power of heaven.

---

15. Deere, *Surprised by the Power*, 44.
16. Finney, *Memoirs*, 21.

Now, perhaps you're thinking, "This is too easy." It's supposed to be. God does the filling, you do the receiving. But you say, "I don't feel anything. I don't feel different." I wonder what Bezalel felt when he was filled with the Spirit and became the best version of himself and his craft. Did he feel any different, or was the evidence in who he was becoming and the talent he was now creating?

Obey—The Spirit fills us not just for personal renewal but for public witness. Acts 1:8 says, "You will receive power . . . and you will be My witnesses." Obedience may sound rigid, but it's not—it's relational. It's about stepping into the divine triangle and walking out a life shaped by a renewed mind and a renovated soul. It's following the biblical pattern of discipleship and experiencing God showing up in unexpected, miraculous ways.

You may discover new boldness and new desires. You may begin to pray differently. See people differently. Love differently. This isn't hype—it's the Spirit resonating within your soul. As you grow, you'll learn to trust his leading and recognize his voice. Prayer becomes a lifeline, not a ritual. Your natural skills and talents will be supernaturally enhanced. Your personality won't be erased—it will be infused with divine purpose.

As John Wimber once said, "Faith is spelled R-I-S-K."[17] Obedience simply means following the Spirit's lead. Taking the next step. Risking where he prompts.

• •

The Spirit never fills us for theory—he fills us for movement.
To obey is to step into risk, to trust that his power will meet
you on the other side of your yes. This is where gatecrashers
are forged and Stockholm fear is broken.

• •

CONCLUSION: THE SPIRIT-FILLED LIFE BEGINS NOW

You don't need to understand everything. You don't need to feel a certain way or compare your experience to anyone else's.

---

17. Wimber and Springer, *Power Evangelism*, 78.

Your gifts will come alive, your faith will grow bold, and your life will become a divine appointment. The same Spirit that hovered over creation, that empowered prophets and kings, that filled Jesus himself, and that ignited the early church, now stands ready to fill you. Right where you are. With all that you are. For all that God has prepared for you.

You've been invited into the fullness of life in the Spirit. Walk in it. Work in it. Worship in it. So breathe deep. Quiet your heart. Flip the breaker.

You are not alone. You are not powerless. You are ready.

Welcome to Stockdale Paradox Christianity. You just made the gates of hell shudder!

THE GATES WON'T HOLD

The Kingdom Triangle Algorithm was never meant to sit framed on the wall of a conference room. It is a battle formation, and battle formations are only useful when the soldiers step forward. We have recovered the apex of the Spirit, renewed our minds, restored our souls, and activated the protocol that unites them.

Now comes the moment the gates of hell fear most: when a fully aligned, Spirit-empowered, mind-sharpened, soul-secured church moves forward in formation.

Section 3 is next, and it's not theoretical; it's a call to impact. From formation to confrontation, we advance as gatecrashers, not gatekeepers, into enemy territory with truth, grace, and courage. The Spirit, who animated Brainerd's prayers and Palau's preaching, empowers us to stand where others bow, choosing Stockdale's resolve over Stockholm's capitulation. "You will receive power . . . and you will be My witnesses" (Acts 1:8). Time to crash the party!

SECTION THREE

Crashing the Gates—Rescuing the Captives

Jesus never said the gates of hell might give way if the church tried hard enough. He said they will not prevail (Matt 16:18). Gates are defensive structures. They don't chase anyone—they keep captives in. The only reason gates are mentioned at all is because the church is supposed to be moving forward. It's our mission to crash them.

For too long, we've lived as if the gates were advancing on us—hiding behind programs, debating culture from a safe distance, and calling it faithfulness. But gates don't march. If they're rattling, it's because God's people are finally pressing against them.

That press is what this section is about. Here we will see what happens when the people of God, aligned in Spirit, mind, and soul, refuse to sit back and let darkness dictate the terms. We will look to models of courageous resistance, count the cost of engagement, and answer the call to live as Stockdale Christians in a Stockholm world.

To help us picture this, creation gives us a huge image: the rhinoceros. And believe it or not, a group of rhinoceroses is called a *crash*. Rhinos have poor eyesight but incredible power. When they run, they cannot see more than thirty feet ahead—but they run anyway, undeterred by what lies beyond their view. When they charge together, they do so as a unified force that flattens anything standing in their way.

That is the church. Not a cautious, isolated spectator of culture, but a Spirit-empowered crash. We are commissioned by the risen Christ to advance his kingdom with boldness and resolve. We are called to storm—not retreat. To crash—not cower. And we do it not in our own strength but by the same Spirit who raised Jesus from the dead (Rom 8:11).

This third and final section of *Stockdale Paradox Christianity* is a clarion call to courageous action. Having exposed the cultural drift, diagnosed the disease of capitulation, and rediscovered the geometry of kingdom living, we now turn toward the battlefield. It's time to act. Time to speak. Time to rise. Together.

WHAT LIES AHEAD IS THIS . . .

Chapter 8, "Sisu: Beyond Grit," explores the Spirit-empowered resilience needed to endure when life feels unbearable. *Sisu* is more than human toughness; it is a holy stubbornness infused with divine strength. Time and again, God has chosen ordinary men and women and filled them with extraordinary courage to press on when retreat seemed easier.

Here we draw on the principle of progressive overload, the way strength is built by adding weight, rep after rep. In the same way, every act of obedience is a spiritual repetition, every risk is resistance, and every prayer is training for the trenches. The soul, like the body, grows stronger under pressure. This is not a grit we manufacture but a holy muscle the Spirit develops in us as we keep showing up, keep lifting, and keep believing.

Sisu fused with the Spirit forms believers who do not bow to fear or fatigue but rise to the challenge with a strength not their own. This chapter calls us to train for the long fight, to welcome the resistance that forges resilience, and to step forward with the unbreakable determination of Spirit-filled saints.

Then in chapter 9, "Standing While Others Bow," we hear the call of the church to courage in an age of compromise and silence. This chapter reminds us that faithfulness has always required standing tall when the world, and sometimes even God's people, choose to kneel to lesser powers. From Daniel in Babylon to Esther in Persia, Scripture gives us portraits of courageous resistance. Today, as Stockholm Syndrome Christianity too often trades conviction for comfort, we need modern disciples who refuse to blend in or bow down. Whether pastor, board member, or pew-sitter, the summons is the same: to rise with Spirit-filled Sisu—a holy resilience that will not bend, will not break, and will not be bought.

Finally, we arrive at chapter 10, "Stockholm or Stockdale . . . the Choice "is" Yours!" This closing chapter is a call to arms, urging us to move beyond

Section Three: Crashing the Gates—Rescuing the Captives

passive religion into the costly path of courageous discipleship. Jesus did not endure the cross so his followers could slip quietly into the culture, attending church once a week and living unnoticed. He died and rose again to ignite a movement, a Spirit-charged force that storms the very gates of hell.

Here, the themes of the Kingdom Triangle, the Stockdale Paradox, and the witness of Scripture converge. The challenge is clear and inescapable: will we settle for Stockholm, cozying up to our captors, or will we rise as Stockdale Christians, realists who face the brutal facts yet cling unshakably to ultimate victory in Christ?

This final chapter re-centers our mission on the Great Commission and calls the church to burn with kingdom fire once more. Yet this is not a halftime pep talk from a coach, but a commissioning from the King. We do not stand in our own strength. The same Spirit who filled the upper room fills us still, empowering us to do exploits for his kingdom. The choice is before us, and the Spirit is everything in making it possible.

Together, these final chapters form a crash—a thundering, Spirit-led advance of God's people into enemy territory. If the church has any hope of transforming culture, it must begin by recovering its courage.

The time for retreat is over. The church was never designed to hunker down behind stained glass and wait out the culture. We are not keepers of the status quo—we are warriors of the in-breaking kingdom. The gates of hell are not assaulting us—we are called to assault them. And now, with grit in our bones and fire in our lungs, it's time to charge.

We are not on defense anymore. We are on the move. Taking back marriages. Reclaiming prodigals. Disrupting lies with truth. Healing the sick. Casting out demons. Preaching the gospel with boldness. Not by might. Not by power. But by the Spirit of the Living God. This is the church militant, not angry but armed. Not bitter but blazing. Not afraid but advancing.

So saddle up, rhinoceroses. Square your shoulders. Grip your spiritual weapons. We may not see all that lies ahead, but we know Who goes before us.

CHAPTER 8

Sisu: Beyond Grit

> Courage is not simply one of the virtues,
> but the form of every virtue at the testing point.
>
> —C. S. Lewis, *Screwtape Letters*

WE ARE NOT CALLED to merely survive—we are called to overcome. The Christian life is not one of passive endurance, but of active, Spirit-empowered perseverance. At the heart of this resilient faith lies a concept that feels foreign to many, but deeply familiar to a few: *Sisu*.

This chapter marks the beginning of our final movement: "Crashing the Gates—Rescuing the Captives." By now, we've diagnosed the cultural drift and exposed the silence of the shepherds. We've reconnected the power cord of the Spirit and come to realize what has been possible all along. The triangle has been energized. Minds are being renewed, empty souls are becoming whole, and the church is waking up. The question is, what now? What does it look like to embody Sisu when cultural winds rage, when allies fall silent, and when comfort beckons louder than conviction?

This is where theory becomes practice, where orthodoxy demands orthopraxy. It's one thing to believe truth; it's another to stand in it when storms rage. That's the essence of Sisu in the kingdom: Spirit-fueled courage and mental resolve in the face of impossible odds.

DEFINING SISU: THE GRIT BENEATH THE ICE

Sisu is a uniquely Finnish term. It cannot be cleanly translated because it is not merely a word—it is a worldview. It is the deep well of inner strength, a fierce determination that rises when others retreat. Sisu is courage without applause, resolve without reassurance, sacrifice without spotlight.

Finnish psychologist Emilia Lahti explains, "Sisu is embodied fortitude, the kind that rises when all strength is spent."[1]

I've witnessed this firsthand through my wife, Leila. Though 100 percent Finnish by blood, she was born in Buenos Aires. After World War II, her family fled there in search of survival. For ten years they petitioned to come to America. Then suddenly, permission was granted—but they had only forty-eight hours to leave. With little money, no time to sell belongings, and only cargo-ship tickets in hand, they set out for Los Angeles in 1962. They arrived with less than two hundred dollars. That's not just immigration—that's Sisu. Quiet resolve. Preparedness over panic. Faith in action without fanfare.

Watching Leila, I came to understand: Sisu is not theory. It's a presence. A practiced persistence. When life gets hard, Leila doesn't panic—she prepares. She doesn't whine—she works. That's Sisu. No fanfare. No spotlight. Just quiet, unwavering faith in action. Her steady resolve became a living parable of the spiritual grit we are all called to cultivate.

It is more than momentary courage. It is sustained, soul-deep stamina in the face of long odds. It is the mindset that pushes forward when the emotional fuel tank hits empty. While the modern West often glorifies comfort and ease, Sisu glories in hardship as the proving ground of character.

Sisu is the opposite of entitlement. It is not a cry for help, but a decision to hold the line. It is the refusal to quit, not because the odds are good but because the calling is clear. It is Stockdale all the way. While similar to Western notions of courage or grit, Sisu carries a more enduring, internal tenacity—a silent strength that doesn't need a stage. It is also distinct from Hebrew *chutzpah*, which often involves boldness, daring, or audacity in the face of risk.

Whereas *chutzpah* might challenge authority or push boundaries, and Western grit might push through with external drive, Sisu is a quiet, immovable fortitude: a mental, moral, and spiritual resolve to persevere, even when no one is watching and when there is no guarantee of reward. It is a

---

1. Lahti, "Sisu," 14.

slow-burning flame that refuses to go out. What grit is to ambition, Sisu is to faithfulness.

FINLAND'S WINTER WAR (1939–1940)

Finland's defense against the Soviet Union is the classic embodiment of Sisu in action. In November 1939, the Soviet Union launched an unprovoked invasion of Finland, expecting a swift and decisive victory against a vastly smaller and poorly equipped neighbor. Outnumbered three to one, outgunned by tanks and planes, and ill-equipped for modern warfare, the Finnish forces responded not with panic, but with gritty resolve. In temperatures that often dropped below −40 degrees Fahrenheit, they relied on intimate knowledge of their terrain, guerrilla tactics, and an iron-willed determination to defend their homeland.

The Finns, many on skis and dressed in winter camouflage, moved like ghosts through the snow-covered forests. Armed with outdated rifles, Molotov cocktails, and little more than hunting gear, they ambushed Soviet tanks, cut off supply lines, and turned the deep snow into an ally. As historian William Trotter notes, "The Red Army came with numbers; the Finns responded with spirit [Sisu]"[2] Military analysts have since described the Finnish resistance as a case study in asymmetric warfare—how resolve and resourcefulness can frustrate even the mightiest of forces.

Soviet leaders believed they would sweep through in days. But they didn't account for Sisu. In the words of Marshal Mannerheim, Finland's military leader, "This war has shown what spiritual strength means for a nation."[3]

The peace treaty that ended the war in March 1940 came at great cost to Finland, but not defeat. The Soviets took territory, but they failed to conquer the spirit of the Finnish people. They may have claimed land, but they could not claim victory. The world took notice. The Finnish people didn't wait for ideal conditions. They had Sisu—and it made all the difference. Leila's father, Pertti Laitio, an Army sharpshooter, was twenty years old in 1939 and part of the Sisu resistance.

This is not merely nationalistic grit. It is a transferable principle. In a world where Christians are tempted to either rage or retreat, Sisu models a third path: resilient presence. To stand when others flee. To remain rooted

---

2. Trotter, *Frozen Hell*, 138.
3. Clements, *Mannerheim*, 144.

when winds howl. To be unbending when pressure demands compromise. To speak truth when your voice shakes. To obey God when the costs rise. To hold the line when no one claps.

Sisu is the marrow-deep conviction that our position is not dictated by popularity, ease, or outcome—but by calling. It is the resolve of Hananiah, Mishael, and Azariah: "Even if he does not deliver us, we will not bow" (see Dan 3:16–18). It is Job's declaration, "Though he slay me, yet will I trust him" (see Job 13:15).

It is not loud, but it is unshakable. It is not flashy, but it is immovable. Sisu may wear a furrowed brow instead of a victory smile, but it is the face of faithful endurance. It is the substance of the saint who shows up, stays faithful, and holds the line long after applause has died down.

In a church culture obsessed with platform and spotlight, Sisu whispers, "Keep going. No one needs to see—God sees." And, as we will discover, when anointed by the Spirit, this quality is not only admirable but essential for the kind of courageous Christianity our times demand.

SISU AND THE SPIRIT: HOLY RESILIENCE

Human Sisu can only go so far. But when fused with the Spirit of God, it becomes holy resilience. Imagine a storm at sea. Waves crash. Wind howls. Lightning forks the sky. Ships capsize. But there in the chaos, a lighthouse stands, unmoved, unfazed, its light cutting through the darkness. That's Sisu, but not merely human Sisu. That's Spirit-filled resilience.

* * *

Sisu without the Spirit is grit that eventually gives way. But Sisu infused with the Spirit becomes holy resilience.

* * *

Throughout the biblical narrative, God raised up men and women who embodied this kind of Spirit-infused Sisu. Paul, for example, endured beatings, imprisonment, and shipwreck. On a storm-tossed sea he stood before terrified sailors and declared, "Therefore, take courage, men, because I believe God that it will be just the way it was told to me" (Acts 27:25). When the ship shattered and he washed up on Malta, a viper fastened onto his hand. The locals thought he would die, but Paul simply shook it into the fire and continued his mission. His resolve was not arrogance—it was assurance born of the Spirit. His life testified that storms and serpents cannot derail a Spirit-driven calling.

Stephen, chosen to serve tables and later to testify before the Sanhedrin, displayed holy Sisu in the face of certain death. Accused falsely, he spoke truth with courage. As stones rained down, he forgave his killers and saw heaven open, Jesus standing to receive him. His Sisu was not human bravado; it was Spirit-filled conviction that reverberated into history, planting seeds in Saul of Tarsus who would later become Paul.

Deborah, prophetess and judge, was more than a single-line heroine in Israel's history. In a time when male leadership faltered, she rose to speak the word of the Lord. She summoned Barak, commanding him to gather ten thousand men to confront Sisera's army, assuring him that God had already given victory (Judg 4:6–7). When Barak hesitated, insisting she go with him, Deborah agreed, knowing it meant the honor of victory would go to a woman. She then sang with Barak a song of triumph (Judg 5), not to celebrate her own boldness but to glorify the God who empowered her to lead. Her Sisu was not about grasping power but about obeying a divine summons when no one else would rise.

Nehemiah's Sisu looked different. He did not fight on a battlefield, but on the construction site of a ruined city. Surrounded by enemies, mocked, threatened, and even betrayed, he kept building. With a sword in one hand and a trowel in the other, he rebuilt Jerusalem's walls. When called to abandon his post, he declared with unshakable resolve, "I am doing a great work and cannot come down" (Neh 6:3). That is Sisu—steady, immovable, Spirit-anointed perseverance.

Esther embodied Sisu in the royal palace. She was not a warrior, but her act of courage changed the destiny of her people. When the decree of death hung over the Jews, she risked her life by entering the king's presence unsummoned. Her words, "If I perish, I perish" (Esth 4:16), were not melodrama but a settled conviction. Clothed in royal robes yet anchored in divine calling, her obedience was more powerful than any edict.

David displayed Sisu long before his famous battle with Goliath. Refusing Saul's heavy armor, he trusted the simple sling and the God who had delivered him from lions and bears. His victory was not about weaponry but about Spirit-born trust.

Likewise, Naomi and Ruth, though broken and displaced, displayed quiet perseverance rooted in faith. Naomi did not sugarcoat her pain, but she did not quit. Ruth, the Moabite widow, embodied stubborn loyalty and immovable Sisu in her vow to Naomi: "Where you go, I will go; your people will be my people, and your God my God" (see Ruth 1:16). Their faithfulness, though quiet and often overlooked, rewrote their destiny and wove them into the very lineage of Christ.

But Rahab's story deserves careful attention. She was a Canaanite prostitute living in Jericho, surrounded by pagan culture and doomed for destruction. Yet when Israel's spies entered her city, she hid them on her rooftop, defying her king and risking execution. Why? She confessed to the spies, "I know that the LORD has given you this land. . . . For the LORD your God is God in heaven above and on the earth below" (Josh 2:9–11). Rahab's Sisu was not born of religious pedigree—it was raw, desperate faith that risked everything on God's promise. She tied a scarlet cord to her window, a symbol of trust in the God she barely knew but fully believed. Her act of courageous loyalty not only saved her household but wove her into the genealogy of Christ as well (Matt 1:5). Spirit-empowered Sisu transformed a marginalized woman into a matriarch of faith.

This holy Sisu runs like a golden thread through church history as well. Corrie ten Boom defied the Nazis by hiding Jews and endured Ravensbrück concentration camp with forgiveness on her lips.

Brother Andrew, known as "God's Smuggler," showed the same Spirit-born Sisu in the twentieth century. He drove a small blue Volkswagen across the borders of Communist countries with his car packed full of Bibles. Countless times guards would stop him, search cars, and miss his contraband. He often prayed, "Lord, when you made blind eyes see, please now make seeing eyes blind."[4] His daring faith was not recklessness but obedience to a call greater than his own safety. Andrew's Sisu was the determination to get God's word into hands that had been starved of it, no matter the danger. He risked arrest, imprisonment, even death, because Spirit-empowered conviction compelled him to act.

Holy resilience is never showy. It may wear armor, robes, or ashes, but it always carries the same fire within. It is the steady conviction that obeys God at all costs. It is Peter and John before the Sanhedrin saying, "We are unable to stop speaking about what we have seen and heard" (Acts 4:20). It is ordinary men and women who become unbreakable because Presence has filled them.

Time and again, God has chosen the unlikely, the overlooked, the ordinary and filled them with extraordinary Sisu—Paul in chains, Deborah in battle, Stephen in martyrdom, Esther in the palace, Ruth in loyalty,

---

4. Brother Andrew, *God's Smuggler*, 134.

Nehemiah on the wall, Rahab in Jericho, Corrie in Ravensbrück, Andrew at the borders. Different settings, same Spirit. Different battles, same backbone. When inner fire is fused with divine presence, mountains move, empires tremble, and the kingdom advances.

From generation to generation, holy Sisu has marked God's people. And now, it is our turn.

•••••••••••••••••••••••••••••••••

The stories of Scripture and history are not given for admiration but imitation. Their endurance is a summons to us—ordinary believers with extraordinary access to the same Spirit who made them unbreakable.

•••••••••••••••••••••••••••••••••

But how does this kind of resilience actually take shape in us? How does an ordinary believer cultivate extraordinary endurance? The answer is not found in sudden heroics but in steady training. Just as muscles only grow under tension, so faith matures through the discipline of resistance, repetition, and rest. This is the pathway of progressive overload—the spiritual gym where holy Sisu is strengthened for the battles ahead.

FROM GRIT TO GLORY: THE PATH OF PROGRESSIVE OVERLOAD

One of the first things I do, three to four days a week, is hit the gym. Though I used to do triathlons decades ago, I'm not much for running. Years in construction left my knees less than thrilled about long jogs or aerobic classes. But weight lifting? That I love. There's something deeply satisfying about challenging yourself against the iron. Stacking the plates, gripping cold steel, and testing yourself against resistance. There's nothing like it.

Muscle growth is a process called hypertrophy. It is the increase in size and strength of muscle fibers as they adapt to the stress and load. That's when I encountered a principle that changed everything: progressive overload—the concept that strength only comes by gradually increasing resistance over time. No challenge, no change. No load, no growth. You have to lift heavier if you want to get stronger.

Sisu: Beyond Grit

Our former Marine son, Adam, hoorah, once gave me a T-shirt that simply read: LFT HVY. At first glance, it's just a gym bro slogan. But the truth behind it is profound: keep pushing, your muscles will adapt. Keep lifting heavier and heavier and you'll be amazed at what you're capable of. That shirt now serves as a quiet creed for my spiritual walk. In Christ, we can do all things. So lift heavy. And the best part? He's spotting you. He's right there—shouldering the strain, lending his strength, making sure the bar doesn't crush you.

But not everyone lifts. You see, progressive overload leads to hypertrophy—muscle expansion and strength through strain. But the opposite happens if we don't. If we refuse the challenge, there's a danger: atrophy. When muscle isn't used, it shrinks. It weakens. It forgets how to carry the weight it once bore with ease. And spiritual atrophy works the same way. When we dodge obedience, avoid risk, or ignore the Spirit's prompts, we lose the strength we once had. Our discernment dulls. Our love wanes. Our courage vanishes.

Sisu doesn't wait for the right conditions. Though tired, sore, and with a full agenda, it still gets up, puts on the gym clothes, and heads off to battle the iron. It rises when conditions are worst. It's not the second wind; it's the resolve to finish the race when you don't believe a second wind is coming. It's the sacred stubbornness to keep lifting, even after failure. And when that Sisu is infused by the Spirit, it becomes something transcendent.

But here's the secret often missed: the weight room is only half the story. Muscle growth doesn't actually happen while you lift. Resistance causes micro-tears in the muscle tissue. It is in the rebuilding process that the muscle doesn't just return to baseline but becomes stronger than before. The real growth occurs during rest and recovery. The lifting simply provides the necessary resistance to signal your body to grow.

In spiritual terms, rest isn't inactivity—it's sacred strategy. Jesus modeled this perfectly. Again and again in the Gospels, we see him withdraw from the crowds, from the disciples, from the demands, to rest before the Father. This wasn't weakness. This was wisdom. Rest is not quitting—it's trusting. It is fasting from doing so that God can do the deeper work in us. In rest, our spirit breathes, recalibrates, and realigns. Amazing things happen in rest, if we'll only stop long enough to notice.

We need to relearn this rhythm. In the gym and in the kingdom. We lift. We rest. We grow. And over time, our spiritual hypertrophy becomes visible—not in physical muscle tone, but in unshakable faith, settled joy, and quiet endurance.

This is where Sisu shines brightest. Not just in the one-off acts of heroic defiance, but in the daily discipline of lifting more than we did the day before. Small Sisu events are still Sisu events. Saying no to temptation, holding your tongue, getting back up when you fall—these are not trivial. They are reps. They are divine micro-decisions that expand our capacity to bear more, stand longer, and go deeper.

Like David before Goliath, it's not about how impressive we look or how seasoned we are. He had no armor, no pedigree, just a sling, five stones, and a soul aflame with conviction: "You uncircumcised Philistine, how dare you insult the God of heaven!" That is sanctified Sisu. That is what it means to take on a challenge well over our pay grade and watch God show up.

The energized Kingdom Triangle—Spirit, mind, and soul—empowers us. We do not pull ourselves up by sheer willpower. We stand in the strength of the Lord and the power of his might (Eph 6:10). The goal is not self-made resilience, but Spirit-formed endurance. And over time, we become battle-tested disciples, lifting more in faith than we ever thought possible.

Faith works in the same way. Every challenge, every hardship, every burden we lift spiritually may tear us slightly, but with rest in God's presence, something deeper forms. Strength. Depth. Power. Small faith lifts are just as valid as the big ones. Don't overdo it—but don't under-do it either. You don't walk into the gym and bench three hundred pounds your first day. And God doesn't expect you to take down Goliath on your first try. But he does want to see if you'll pick up the sling.

Progressive overload, whether physical or spiritual, is about capacity-building. And Sisu is what keeps you coming back. There was a T-shirt hanging in the window of a gym in Smithville, Texas, where Leila and I were grabbing breakfast. It said, "I hate this place . . . see you tomorrow!" That's Sisu. The gritty resolve to keep going. Keep pushing. Keep trusting. The quiet fire that says, "Not today, devil. I'm still here . . . see you tomorrow."

• •

As the weight increases, so will our strength. Obedience becomes a rep, risk becomes resistance, and prayer becomes training. This is progressive overload in the Spirit—where Sisu is forged and the church becomes a gatecrashing force.

• •

For the follower of Jesus, that's precisely where the Spirit enters in. As Paul wrote, "When I am weak, then I am strong" (2 Cor 12:10). God doesn't despise weakness—he builds strength in its soil. Through the progressive overload of grace, something supernatural begins to form: hypertrophy of the soul.

This is not just for survival. It's for battle. And it's not a battle we fight in the flesh. We press forward with kingdom hypertrophy—resilience formed through resistance, power formed through surrender, and momentum forged through daily obedience.

The Christian life isn't about playing it safe. It's about picking up your cross and pushing into resistance. It's about tearing so we can be rebuilt stronger. And that strength isn't just for survival—it's for battle. The gates of hell won't yield to atrophied Christians. But they will tremble when the church comes crashing in under the explosive force of Spirit-empowered Sisu.

LEILA'S LEGACY: SISU IN THE BLOODLINE

Earlier in this chapter, I introduced you to my Finnish wife, Leila—a modern-day parable of Sisu in the flesh. But the legacy runs even deeper. Her Finnish roots are not simply cultural—they are spiritual. Her family's endurance through difficulty, her habit of preparation over panic, her quiet confidence in God's sovereignty—these aren't personality quirks. They are generational courage, passed down and anointed for such a time as this.

Obviously I have a lot of T-shirts. Leila bought me one that read, "Pray for me . . . I'm married to a Finn." She meant it in jest, but there's truth in it. As a Finn, she knows full well she's got a backbone and drive of steel. And she knows I need prayer! Her tenacity, her clarity of purpose, and her unyielding resolve are unmatched. I'm Norwegian, so together we're both stubborn Vikings, but it's her Sisu that often leads the charge. Her relentless faith and determination have become the engine that drives our shared resolve and passion.

But this legacy isn't limited to bloodlines and ancestry. As believers, we too have a Sisu bloodline—not one passed through DNA, but through divine adoption. We are children of God, heirs with Christ. The same Spirit that raised Jesus from the dead now lives in us (Rom 8:11). It's in our blood, not by birth but by rebirth.

And this is the critical insight: the disconnected triangle had many of us doing all the work ourselves, pulling and striving and dragging our spiritual lives forward by sheer effort. But now that the Spirit has reconnected the system, we see it clearly. All along, the power was available. The triangle wasn't meant to function on human effort but divine energy. We are not called to white-knuckled faith; we are called to Spirit-driven endurance.

Leila's legacy reminds me every day that Sisu isn't just a Finnish trait—it's a kingdom trait. It's what happens when a Spirit-filled life refuses to bow, refuses to quit, and refuses to back down. And through her, I've come to believe with fresh conviction: Sisu runs in the bloodline of every adopted son and daughter of the King.

THE SPIRIT-STRENGTHENED LIFE

To live by Sisu in the kingdom is not to grit your teeth and fake your way through trials. It is to walk through fire and not be burned, to face the storm and still lay bricks for the kingdom. It is resilience laced with revelation, knowing not just what you're made of, but who lives inside you.

This kind of life isn't a matter of personality, toughness, or temperament. It is the product of a life saturated in the Spirit of God. Without him, Sisu eventually breaks. But with him, it bends without snapping, weeps without quitting, fights without fanfare, and endures without applause.

Daniel gives us a striking model of this. Though elevated to a high position within government, he lived constantly under scrutiny from jealous detractors. When a trap was set, designed specifically to exploit his devotion to prayer, Daniel didn't flinch. He knew exactly what it meant. But rather than hide, he flung wide the windows for all to see. He prayed openly, defiantly, but not out of rebellion—out of identity. His Sisu resolve had long been settled: "I will not defile myself." He always presented who he was and Who he represented. In essence, he declared, "I only bow to One—and I will stand against all the rest!"

We need Spirit-saturated Sisu, not just self-help grit. The Stockdale Paradox reminds us to confront the brutal facts yet never lose faith in final victory. That paradox is resolved in Pentecost power. As Paul says, "I am able to do all things through Him who strengthens me" (Phil 4:13).

Sisu: Beyond Grit

TRAINING FOR THE TRENCHES

So how do we develop this holy Sisu? The answer lies in the trenches—not the spotlight. We don't prepare for battle on stages; we prepare in silence, in faithfulness, in repetition. Like the principle of progressive overload in training, we grow by lifting what we can today, then resting in him so we can lift more tomorrow.

Hebrews 11 gives us the great cloud of witnesses, those who lived and died with Sisu in their soul. Abraham stepped into the unknown. Moses chose mistreatment over palace comfort. Gideon faced armies with torches and jars. Rahab trusted a red cord over stone walls. Each one started where they were, and God met them with power. Their lives are not museum relics; they are road signs, cheering us on: "Don't stop. Don't bow. Don't back down."

Progressive overload means we don't start by carrying the cross up the hill, we start by picking it up. It's not about bravado. It's about consistency. It's about showing up for spiritual reps even when no one sees.

As I've experienced firsthand in the gym, muscles don't grow during the lift—they grow in recovery. The weight provides the stimulus, but the body responds in rest. The same is true of faith. God doesn't waste the resistance. Every hard thing is producing something in you, if you stay in the fight.

- *Start with surrender.* Invite the Spirit to empower your perseverance.
- *Embrace the resistance.* Hard things grow strong souls.
- *Practice discipline.* Sisu is forged in ordinary faithfulness.
- *Choose courage over comfort.* Follow the Lamb even when he leads to Calvary.
- *Stay in the fight.* The gate-crashing army doesn't retreat.

This is not a call to masochism. It is a call to mission. To live beyond grit is to live with Spirit-infused Sisu. When grit meets grace, the gates of hell don't stand a chance.

Let the church arise, not in its own strength but in the power of the Spirit. The time for passive discipleship has passed. The time for courageous Christianity is now.

And as we prepare to stand while others bow, remember this: Daniel had settled it in his heart before the lion's den ever opened. Resolve isn't built in the moment of crisis; it's forged in the quiet commitment to walk with God day after day. We will need that kind of Sisu: sanctified, tested, and ready for the days ahead.

The church was never called to survive the culture. It was called to shake it. But you can't shake a world you've been trained to tiptoe around. If the muscles of faith remain unused, they will shrivel in the face of conflict. But if we submit to the Spirit's progressive overload, something powerful begins to happen: our inner being is strengthened with might (Eph 3:16), and the gates of hell will not withstand the pressure of a church that's done playing defense.

We were not designed to sit in pews and shrink. We were built to crash gates.

So . . . LFT HVY!

CHAPTER 9

Standing While Others Bow

> The hottest fire of the furnace is not as hot as the fire
> in the heart of a man who will not bow.
>
> —Anonymous martyr, Eusebius's *Ecclesiastical History*

It's easy to stand when everything is going according to plan, when the setting is comfortable, the surroundings familiar, and the direction certain. But what happens when the plan is shattered, when comfort is stripped away, and you find yourself on a road you never wanted, heading straight into Babylon? Will you still stand then?

When I was nineteen, I was on a Middle East field trip with YWAM (Youth With A Mission). I was staring down the barrel of an AK-47—literally. A Russian soldier had it pointed directly at me, demanding I empty my pockets. I had been tasked with driving a 1974 Chevy Blazer for our team, which we used for supply runs after our bus of fifty-five students reached our camping destinations. I was also the one responsible for the paperwork at each border crossing for the vehicle.

This time, we were in Russia. And I knew I was in possession of illegal copies of the Gospel of John, printed in Russian. As the guards searched the vehicle and began discovering more and more of them, the tension escalated. More guards arrived, and their fury intensified. When they asked if I had any more and I said no, the guard raised his rifle and barked, "Empty your pockets."

In my back right pocket were two more copies.

I emptied my other pockets slowly, heart pounding but strangely calm. He stared me down and shouted again, "More!" I thought, "Okay, God—now would be a great time to show up."

I reached into my back pocket, pulled out the two small Gospels, and laid them on the passenger seat. His grip on the trigger tightened, but after a pause, they took the materials, left a single guard behind to watch me, and confiscated all the Gospels and my personal belongings.

What I cannot explain was the peace: a holy presence that wrapped around me in that moment. No fear. No panic. Just unexplainable calm and total solidarity with the Spirit. They returned, gave back my belongings (minus the Gospels), and forced me to sign a document barring me from ever returning to the country. A guard was assigned to ride the bus with us for the remainder of our trip.

That guard? She gave her life to Jesus before the week was over.

God can and will use us, even in the most tense, inescapable situations, if we simply trust the leading of the Spirit. When the plan is disrupted, when logic fails, when fear should win—the Spirit does not flinch.

The real test isn't your resolve when peace surrounds you; it's your posture when pressure mounts. The Stockdale Christian acknowledges the brutal facts of their situation and, with Spirit-empowered Sisu coursing through their veins, stands anyway. Against all odds. Against overwhelming pressure. Against the pull to bow, blend in, or back down.

That is the true litmus test of faith.

Whatever turn life takes, the Stockdale Christian faces it with quiet, unflinching resolve, to go through, over, under, or forward by any means necessary, empowered by the Spirit and anchored in truth. It's when you're the only one left standing—and yet, you still stand.

In a world saturated with compromise, capitulation, and cultural conformity, the follower of Jesus is called to a bold alternative: standing while others bow.

But take heart; you are not alone. The same Spirit who empowered prophets, apostles, and reformers is alive in you. Whether you're a pastor behind the pulpit, a board member in the back row, or a quiet servant in the pew, this chapter is a call to remember: Spirit-filled Sisu isn't just for heroes or history books—it's for you. For your family. For your ministry. For your neighborhood. God has assigned you a post on the wall, and no one else can fill it. Rise up with the specific gift God has placed within your heart and engage the battle before you. You don't need a spotlight or a stage—you need surrender. You don't need a platform—you need power. This is your moment to stand: not by might, not by power, but by his Spirit.

· ·

The measure of faith is not taken when the crowd applauds, but when the furnace roars. To stand while others bow is not arrogance—it is allegiance. It is the Spirit's fire in the soul refusing to be extinguished by fear.

· ·

PROFILES IN RESISTANCE: THEN AND NOW

The gates of hell are real and the lives of God's people prove they can be breached. As Russ Taff declared in "Not Gonna Bow," on his *Medals* album, we too refuse to bend or give in to the idols of our age. That anthem still rings true today. May it be the soundtrack of a rising generation who refuses to bow, refuses to be silenced, and refuses to surrender their Spirit-filled assignment to the pressures of this age. And know this, we are not the first to sing it.

From Scripture to church history, courageous men and women have stood when others bowed. Their stories are not just history—they are blueprints for our moment:

- Daniel in Babylon refused assimilation, choosing prayer over compromise even at the cost of the lion's den.
- Esther in Persia risked everything to intercede for her people, proving that one surrendered life can shift the fate of a nation.
- Stephen in Jerusalem proclaimed Christ in the face of hostility, trading stones for a crown of glory.
- Deborah in Israel led with courage in a culture that told her to be silent, declaring the Lord had already gone before his people.

And beyond Scripture, history offers a chorus of witnesses:

- Polycarp of Smyrna stood unflinching before Rome, refusing to curse Christ after eighty-six years of faithfulness.

- Perpetua of Carthage, a young mother, faced the beasts of the arena with unshakable resolve, writing in her diary that her true identity was secure in Christ.
- Athanasius of Alexandria stood *contra mundum*, "against the world," defending the deity of Christ when nearly all around him capitulated.
- Jan Hus confronted corruption in the church, sealing his protest with fire.
- Harriet Tubman defied the machinery of slavery, leading captives into freedom guided by visions and prayer.
- Richard Wurmbrand endured torture under Communism, yet emerged as a global voice for persecuted believers.

Each, in their own way, embodied the Stockdale Paradox, facing brutal realities without losing hope. Their resistance proves that standing is always possible when the Spirit empowers ordinary people.

But their stories also reveal a sobering truth: for every Daniel or Wurmbrand who stood, there were multitudes who bowed. Resistance is not the default posture of the church. Without the Spirit's fire, compromise becomes comfortable. With him, courage becomes contagious.

Their gates looked different, but they were real: idolatry in Babylon, corruption in the medieval church, chains on the Underground Railroad, torture chambers under Communism. Yet in every age, God raised up men and women who refused to bow. They named the gates for what they were and stood firm until they fell. And that same Spirit calls us now. The gates of hell are not relics of history; they are visible in our headlines, classrooms, legislatures, and even our pulpits. If they could be breached then, they can be breached now.

CRASHING THE GATES ... RESCUING THE CAPTIVES

We cannot engage what we refuse to recognize. Too many in the church have floated along with the cultural tide, unaware that the temperature is rising—slowly, deceptively, like the parable of the boiling frog. If we will not name the gates of hell, we will never feel the urgency to crash them. But we must always remember why we crash: not to flex strength, but to free the captives. Let's name some of the gates:

The Gate of Ideological Stronghold

These are not harmless debates about language and identity—they are lies with real victims. A school in Vermont knows this firsthand. When Mid Vermont Christian refused to let their girls' basketball team play against a boys' team in disguise, they were expelled from the entire state athletic league.[1] Decades of faithful competition wiped away in an instant, all because they refused to bow to the new idol of gender confusion. Picture those young women who trained and prayed, now told they were unworthy to play unless they denied the reality of God's design. That's what darkness does: it demands surrender, punishes conviction, and mocks truth. And yet, in saying no, they said yes to Christ. They lost trophies but gained a testimony. They showed us what gate-crashing looks like—faithfulness that refuses to yield, even when the price is high.

The Gate of Governmental Overreach

Scripture tells us to honor governing authorities (Rom 13), but when rulers demand what belongs to God, obedience to Christ comes first. We've already discussed Daniel, Esther, and Stephen. We know how they refused to bow. Today, pastors face similar pressure. Some are told to sanitize their sermons, avoid "controversial" topics, or lose favor with tax collectors and cultural elites. To stand in these moments is not rebellion for rebellion's sake; it is allegiance to the higher throne. It is to say, like Peter and John, "We must obey God rather than men" (Acts 5:29). This gate yields not to rage but to Spirit-anchored courage, a courage that will not bow, will not capitulate, and will not lend its voice to the false narratives of the age.

The Gate of Cultural Corruption

This may be the most seductive. It whispers that sin is freedom and brokenness is art. Abortion is paraded as empowerment. Pornography is packaged as liberation. Violence and greed are applauded as entertainment. This is the gate that numbs conscience until people laugh at what God weeps over. But here too, light must enter. The church cannot mirror culture's idols; she must embody holiness and compassion as a radiant alternative. Gate-crashing here means not only saying no to the darkness but offering the

---

1. Rosenberg, "Mid Vermont Christian School."

world something better: the joy of purity, the dignity of life, the beauty of faithfulness.

The Gate of Educational Indoctrination

The classroom, once a place for shaping character and learning truth, has become a battlefield for young hearts and minds. Children are told their identity is fluid, their faith is a relic, and their future belongs to the state. Every assignment, every policy, every textbook whispers, "Trust us, not your parents. Believe us, not your God." This is not neutral—it is a hostile takeover of the next generation. Crashing this gate means discipling our children in the truth, modeling courage at home, and raising them to stand in Babylon without bowing to its idols.

The Gate of Religious Compromise

But not all the gates stand outside the church. The gate of religious compromise yawns wide within. Some pulpits trade prophetic fire for cultural applause. Leaders shave the sharp edges off Scripture so their crowds don't shrink. Worship is designed to entertain rather than transform. The result is a church that looks alive but is dead inside. And yet, even here, the call is clear: leaders must answer to God, not to popularity polls. Silence in the face of sin is complicity. The watchman who refuses to blow the trumpet has blood on his hands. Crashing this gate means restoring fear of the Lord to the pulpit and fire of the Spirit to the altar.

The Gate of Apathy and Lovelessness

And then there is the most insidious gate of all: apathy and lovelessness. No soldiers guard it. No politicians enforce it. It is guarded only by indifference, shrugging shoulders, distracted minds, cold hearts. This is Laodicea all over again: lukewarm, complacent, convinced they are rich while they are poor, blind, and naked. And yet here is the truth: apathy is deadly because it paralyzes the church from within. It convinces believers that their silence is harmless, that their passivity is neutral. But neutrality is not love—it is surrender. Crashing this gate means rekindling love for Christ and love for the lost. It means remembering that the people trapped behind every lie are not the enemy—they are captives needing a gatecrasher.

This is the heart of our mission. We don't crash gates to destroy people but to rescue them. When Jesus sat with the woman at the well, he didn't affirm her brokenness—but he didn't condemn her either. He spoke truth with love, unmasking her thirst and offering living water. That single Spirit-directed conversation turned a sinner into a witness and a village into a mission field. That's what crashing gates looks like: truth that confronts, love that redeems, and a Savior who still sets captives free.

WHEN SILENCE BECOMES SURRENDER

There is a silence more dangerous than outright opposition. It is the silence of pulpits that once thundered truth but now whisper safe platitudes. It is the quiet of watchmen who see danger coming and fold their arms. It is the sound of churches choosing comfort over confrontation, applause over obedience.

For years, pastors excused their silence by pointing to the Johnson Amendment, claiming they could not speak on cultural or political issues without risking their tax status. But that excuse has evaporated. The IRS itself has clarified: sermons, teaching, and discipleship are not campaign activity.[2] The muzzle was never real—it was self-imposed. If pulpits are quiet now, it is not because they must be but because they choose to be.

••••••••••••••••••••••••••••••••••

Silence in the face of deception is not discretion—it is betrayal. A watchman without a trumpet leaves the city exposed, and both shepherd and sheep fall together.

••••••••••••••••••••••••••••••••••

Picture the watchman Ezekiel saw on the wall. If he saw the sword coming and failed to sound the trumpet, the blood of the people was on his hands. That is the weight of silence. A pastor who will not preach the whole counsel of God because he fears empty seats or angry emails has bowed—not to Caesar, but to self-preservation.

---

2. Raymond, "Churches Can Endorse."

And the cost is staggering: Congregations lulled to sleep while culture burns. Children catechized more by TikTok than by the word. Communities collapsing into chaos while churches polish their programs. The world does not need more motivational speeches. It needs prophetic fire.

This is why silence is not neutrality. It is surrender. And surrender is not an option. The pulpit must not bow to Caesar. It must not bow to culture. It must not bow to comfort. It must stand under the weight of the word of God, filled with the fire of the Spirit, and declare, "Thus says the Lord."

The hour demands shepherds who will warn, leaders who will equip, and saints who will shine. If the trumpet does not sound, who will be ready for battle? If the church does not speak, who will tell the truth? If the watchman does not stand, who will protect the city?

This is not a time for timid sermons or domesticated pulpits. It is a time for Spirit-filled voices who know that courage is obedience, that faithfulness is love, and that silence in the face of lies is nothing less than treason against heaven.

SO WE MUST . . .

The evidence has been laid before us. History has shown us men and women who stood when the world bowed. Scripture has given us patterns of resistance, from Daniel's prayers in Babylon to Stephen's cry in Jerusalem. We have seen the gates exposed in our own time: ideologies that demand surrender, governments that overreach, pulpits that go quiet, cultures that corrupt, and apathy that numbs. The question is no longer whether the gates exist. The question is, Will we stand before them, or bow to them?

Our answer begins and ends with Jesus. He is the original Gatecrasher. When his disciples cowered behind locked doors, he stepped into their fear, breathed peace into their panic, and showed them his scars. In an instant, cowards became witnesses. The hunted became the hunters. Game on.

Wherever he walked, the gates trembled. Lepers healed. Demons fled. Outcasts restored. Hypocrisy exposed. Dignity reclaimed. He was not controlled by the crowds, manipulated by the powerful, or silenced by fear. He stood in Spirit-filled authority, declaring the kingdom of God in the face of hell's resistance. And then he turned to us: "As the Father has sent Me, I also send you" (John 20:21).

Standing While Others Bow

That commission was not symbolic. It was literal. He breathed his Spirit into his followers, and at Pentecost the wind and fire came, not to decorate the church but to ignite it. Without him, they hid. With him, they stormed into the streets. They turned the world upside down because the Spirit turned them inside out.

And nothing has changed. The same Spirit who filled Peter on Pentecost fills us today. The same fire that emboldened Stephen burns in us. The same power that raised Jesus from the dead dwells in every believer who surrenders. Stockdale Christians are not fearless by nature; they are fearless by filling. They stand because he stands in them.

So we must move. We cannot sit in locked rooms when resurrection power has been unleashed. We cannot bow to idols already trampled underfoot. We cannot whisper apologies when the Lion of Judah has roared. To see Jesus is to stand. To be filled with his Spirit is to advance. To follow him is to crash the gates until every captive is free.

This is not grit alone. This is holy Sisu: Spirit-filled, Spirit-empowered, Spirit-deployed. And let us remember: people are never the enemy. They are the prize. The very ones shouting the lies are the captives Christ died to rescue. The gate may wear a human face, but behind those eyes is a soul made in God's image. Our war is not against flesh and blood, but against the powers that enslave flesh and blood. That is why we stand: to confront lies, to set captives free, to love as Jesus loved.

The time for neutrality is over. The lines are drawn. The verdict is demanded.

Will you bow to fear, or will you stand in faith?

Will you settle for Stockholm, or will you rise with Stockdale?

The court of heaven is watching. History is waiting. The gates are before us. The Spirit is within us. The choice is yours.

While others bow, may we be found standing.

CHAPTER 10

Stockholm or Stockdale . . . the Choice is Yours!

> You must never confuse faith that you will prevail in the end . . . with the discipline to confront the most brutal facts of your current reality.
>
> —James Stockdale, *Courage Under Fire*

THE CASE HAS BEEN made. The witnesses have testified. The evidence has been laid out. Scripture, history, and even our own headlines have paraded before the stand. Now the jury is in session—and you are sitting in the box. Neutrality is no longer an option. You cannot unhear what has been declared. You cannot unsee what has been revealed. The only question left is this: What verdict will you render with your life?

THE SPIRIT-RESISTANT CHRISTIAN: WHEN FEAR PARALYZES FAITH

Not all who bow do so before idols of gold. Some bow quietly in the pews, paralyzed by fear, doubt, and a low view of the Holy Spirit's power. These are Stockholm Syndrome Christians, captives who have grown comfortable in their chains.

They believe in Jesus but live as if the Spirit were absent. They affirm the creeds but deny the fire. They've traded the upper room for an hour in a pew, delaying obedience while waiting for a safer time.

The Spirit-led life isn't for the super-spiritual elite. It's for every believer—bold or broken, seasoned or struggling. The same Spirit who filled Peter at Pentecost and Stephen at his stoning longs to fill ordinary disciples today. But many have been conditioned to believe the lie, "God can't use someone like me." And so fear calcifies. Pulpits grow hesitant. Congregations grow silent. What begins in leadership echoes in the pew. The result is a Stockholm church that conforms instead of confronts.

POWERLESS CURES AND SPIRITLESS STRATEGIES

This captivity has been diagnosed. John G. West, in *Stockholm Syndrome Christianity*, rightly described how churches often align with the very cultural forces they were sent to resist. Fear of man, desire for acceptance, and spiritual compromise have muzzled pulpits and paralyzed pews. His diagnosis is urgent and needed.

But his cure is incomplete. West names the symptoms—listening to the wrong voices, tolerating compromise, chasing applause—but then prescribes principles without power. Tips, warnings, strategies . . . but no ignition. Not once does he invoke the Holy Spirit as the source of courage and change.

Stockholm cannot be broken by strategies. It can only be shattered by Pentecost. The early church did not rise on clever methods. Peter went from coward to preacher because fire fell (Acts 2). Stephen faced the stones unflinching because he was "filled with the Spirit" (Acts 7:55). The Spirit changes people, not just how they preach but how they perceive reality. Not just what they say but what they carry. Without him, all reform is an empty framework. With him, everything is possible.

This is what's missing from so many well-meaning appeals to action: the wind and fire of Pentecost. The church has settled for a form of godliness without power (2 Tim 3:5). We offer tips instead of transformation. Wisdom without wind. Courage without combustion.

The church doesn't need another clever plan—it needs fire. Without the Spirit's flame, we are workshops of theory; with him, we are battalions of power. Every generation must decide whether to settle for form or to burn with fire.

The Spirit does not fill us for observation but for confrontation. Every believer, every church, every generation must decide: Stockholm or

Stockdale? Ghosting or gatecrashing? Every story ends somewhere—but not every ending is victorious.

A few weeks ago, I opened my mailbox to find something I hadn't seen in years: a jury summons. Like every citizen, I was being called to appear in superior court and fulfill my civic duty. I didn't ask for it. I didn't schedule it. But the summons had come, and ignoring it wasn't an option. My responsibility was clear: show up, hear the case, weigh the evidence, and render a verdict.

That is exactly where we are now. This chapter is our summons. We have been called into the courtroom of eternity to review the case, examine the evidence, and face the facts.

THE CROSSROADS

That brings us here—our moment of decision. The fork in the road is not theoretical; it is standing right in front of us. The wide road of Stockholm bows quietly, survives safely, and dies silently. The narrow road of Stockdale stands boldly, suffers faithfully, and overcomes gloriously.

The arguments have been laid out. The witnesses have testified. The evidence has been presented. The Spirit is still moving. Now the gavel falls, and the verdict must be rendered—not with words, but with your life. The only action left is deliberation.

THE FORK IN THE ROAD

The gates have been exposed. The case is airtight. Now the jury rises to deliberate. This is no longer theory, it is verdict time.

History always comes down to these moments. Israel stood on the plains of Moab, with Moses thundering, "I have set before you life and death, blessing and curse. Choose life" (Deut 30:19). Elijah stood on Mount Carmel, confronting the people with, "How long will you hesitate between two opinions? If Yahweh is God, follow Him. But if Baal, follow him" (1 Kgs 18:21). Jesus stood before his disciples and declared, "Enter through the narrow gate. For the gate is wide and the road is broad that leads to destruction, and there are many who go through it. How narrow is the gate and difficult the road that leads to life, and few find it" (Matt 7:13–14).

The time for decision is now. Like Israel, Elijah's generation, and Jesus' disciples, we stand at a crossroads. Two roads lie before us.

The first is wide. It is polished and popular, lined with the banners of tolerance and self-expression. It promises relevance, acceptance, and applause. It feels noble, even compassionate. But beneath the surface it is Stockholm Christianity: hostages cozying up to their captors, muzzling their witness, blending into the shadows. It is the road of compromise and captivity, the broad path where truth bends and souls wither.

The second is narrow. It is rugged, costly, and marked by scars. Few choose it, and those who do often walk with tears in their eyes and crosses on their backs. But it is the only road that sets captives free. This is Stockdale Christianity: realists who face the brutal facts, yet cling unshakably to victory in Christ. It is not a path of human grit alone, but of Spirit-fueled Sisu, where resilience is ignited by fire from heaven. This road topples giants. This road crashes gates. This road rescues captives.

Make no mistake, the verdict cannot be delayed. Neutrality is a myth. Every step you take leans toward one road or the other. Stockholm offers comfort but ends in chains. Stockdale demands courage but ends in crowns. Stockholm seeks survival but forfeits the Spirit. Stockdale embraces the Spirit and advances the kingdom.

The case has been made. The evidence is overwhelming. God's word is true. His Spirit is power. His Son has already triumphed. And now the gavel rests in your hand.

So choose. Choose truth over lies. Choose righteousness over compromise. Choose the honor of God over the applause of men. Choose the Spirit's fire over hollow forms. Choose to stand when others bow.

Choose carefully. Because whichever road you take will not only define your story—it will shape the future of those who follow in your steps.

• •

The road you choose is never walked alone. Your steps carve a path for your children, your church, your community. Stockholm shrinks the horizon to self-preservation; Stockdale stretches it toward eternal impact. Which trail of footprints will you leave?

• •

Because there is only one power that can break chains, crash gates, and set captives free—the power of the Holy Spirit. And there is only one road that leads there.

But not everyone chooses that road. Many hear the truth, nod their heads, even admire the courage of others, yet drift back into captivity. They don't renounce Christ; they simply settle for survival. This is the Stockholm temptation.

THE STOCKHOLM TEMPTATION: CHOOSING COMFORT OVER CALLING

Not all Christians deny Christ outright. Some simply stay silent. They ghost the Spirit, ghost holiness, ghost courage—until all that remains is an echo chamber of compromise dressed in Christian language.

It often looks respectable. Silence disguised as wisdom. Capitulation masked as compassion. Compromise justified as relevance. They sing about surrender on Sunday, but bow to culture on Monday. They applaud sermons that mention truth in passing, but shrink when it demands obedience. They keep peace at the dinner table, but abandon it in the public square.

At its heart, Stockholm Christianity is not about open rebellion—it is about survival. Keep your reputation intact. Keep the applause of peers. Keep the illusion of faith without the offense of the cross. But survival is not the same as salvation. Jesus never said, "Play it safe and you'll live." He said, "Deny yourself, take up your cross daily, and follow me" (see Luke 9:23).

The subtle danger is this: Stockholm Christianity doesn't feel like apostasy. It feels like balance. It feels like wisdom. It feels like keeping doors open. But slowly, it drains the church of conviction, courage, and power until what remains is little more than a powerless shell with a Christian label.

This is the wide road Jesus warned us about. It is broad, it is easy, and it ends in destruction. Stockholm Christianity whispers, "Blend in. Be nice. Don't make waves."

But Jesus didn't call us to blend. He called us to blaze. He called us to live as light in the darkness, salt in the decay, truth in the confusion, courage in the face of fear. He never promised safety. He promised a cross. Yet in that cross is power, freedom, and joy.

So the invitation is clear: don't settle for comfort when Christ offers calling. Don't mistake silence for wisdom, or survival for faithfulness. Don't ghost the Spirit when he is ready to fill you, gift you, and use you.

STOCKHOLM OR STOCKDALE ... THE CHOICE IS YOURS!

THE STOCKDALE CALL: HOPE WITH EYES WIDE OPEN

Stockdale Christians are not naïve. They don't deny the darkness—they defy it with light. They see the warfare for what it is, yet they rise anyway, clinging to Christ, not to comfort.

And they don't all look the same. Some wear robes and preach in pulpits. Most wear jeans, aprons, or uniforms and go unnoticed by the world. Yet heaven notices. And hell notices too.

A mother kneels at her child's bedside, sowing prayers deeper than any TikTok trend could uproot. A teacher quietly chooses truth over tenure, refusing to echo lies even if it costs her. A grocery clerk blesses every customer under her breath, planting seeds of the kingdom in aisle three. A mechanic prays over busted engines and busted lives, laying hands on both. A businessman resists the urge to cut corners and instead funds kingdom work in secret. A student opens her Bible in a hostile classroom and discovers that courage spreads.

These are not superstars. They are not the famous few. They are ordinary disciples who believe the Spirit meant it when he said he would pour himself out on all flesh. And when he fills them—courage ignites. Chains snap. Fear flees.

Stockdale Christians carry scars, but they also carry songs. They may be mocked, misunderstood, or marginalized, but they refuse to bow. They know survival is not the goal—faithfulness is. And faithfulness, fueled by the Spirit, always overcomes.

And here is the good news: this life is not reserved for the elite. It is not only for the missionaries, martyrs, or giants of church history. It is for you. For the hesitant dad. For the weary pastor. For the overlooked teenager. For the doubting grandmother. For anyone willing to trade Stockholm silence for Stockdale surrender.

It is possible because the same Spirit who filled Peter at Pentecost, who steadied Stephen under the stones, who transformed Saul the persecutor into Paul the proclaimer, has been poured out on you. What he did in the upper room, he is still doing in living rooms, classrooms, and break rooms. You do not have to summon this courage on your own. You need only yield to the One who already lives within you.

The narrow road is not empty. It is crowded with saints who have walked before you, walk beside you, and will walk after you. And the same Spirit who gave them strength will give it to you.

So step forward. Lift your head. Grip the cross. Fix your eyes. Take the narrow road. Because the gates of hell don't fall to the famous—they fall to the faithful.

DECLARATION OF THE STOCKDALE CHRISTIAN

This is what it means to walk the narrow road. Not perfection. Not prominence. But ordinary disciples marked by Spirit-filled courage and faithfulness that shakes the gates of hell.

Yet we need more than scattered stories—we need a movement. A people who refuse to bow. A family of believers who live with open eyes and burning hearts. What follows is not just a description—it's a call to rise.

We are not looking for comfortable Christians. We are not looking for crowd-pleasers or cultural chameleons. We are looking for Stockdale Christians—disciples forged in fire, formed in truth, and filled with the Spirit of the Living God.

They are the ones who walk steady when the world shakes. Their joy doesn't evaporate when headlines grow darker; in fact, it shines brighter because they know resurrection is not just a doctrine; it's their destiny. Fear still knocks at their door, but it never gets the keys. Hope carries them forward even when logic says all is lost. Truth flows from their lips with tenderness that disarms cynicism and with conviction that cannot be bought. Their love is costly, inconvenient, and unconcerned with applause.

You can spot them in the storm. When others scatter, they remain. When others bow, they stand taller. They take hits and keep moving. They fall, but they rise again—because there is a power within them that refuses to quit. Their prayers are not polite recitations but battle cries, shaping outcomes in unseen realms long before results show up on earth. The enemy knows their names. Hell trembles when they wake up in the morning.

And here is the secret: these are not superheroes. They are not chosen for their pedigree or platform. They are ordinary people—mothers and grandfathers, students and laborers, teachers and truck drivers—who have simply said yes to the Spirit's fire.

This is not extremism. It is not arrogance. It is allegiance. It is obedience. It is courage baptized in the Spirit and aimed at the glory of Christ.

And it is possible for you—yes, you. This is not a distant ideal. It is what you were born again to be. It is what Jesus meant when he said,

"Follow me." The Spirit is ready to make you into more than a survivor. He is ready to make you into a warrior.

This is the declaration, not for the few, but for all who dare to believe that Pentecost was just the beginning.

BEYOND HUMAN RESILIENCE

Admiral James Stockdale showed us the heights of human grit—surviving torture, defying despair, clinging to honor against impossible odds. His story inspires us. Yet as noble as his resilience was, it reached only so far. Sheer willpower can endure a prison camp, but it cannot storm the gates of hell.

And this is where the church must stand apart. What Stockdale modeled through grit, we are called to multiply through grace. We are indwelt by the Spirit of the Living God. What is possible in the natural becomes unstoppable in the supernatural. We are not summoned merely to survive with dignity; we are commissioned to advance with power.

This is the revolution of the Kingdom Triangle, fully energized: a mind renewed in truth, a soul restored in wholeness, and a life ablaze with the Spirit's fire. Courage without clarity collapses. Courage without character corrupts. Courage without power is futility. But when Spirit, mind, and soul converge, the gates of hell cannot stand.

"'Not by strength or by might, but by My Spirit,' says the LORD of Armies" (Zech 4:6).

THIS IS THE REVOLUTION WE NEED

The church does not need another manual, another program, or another strategy. We need fire. We need an outpouring of the Spirit that shakes pulpits, classrooms, boardrooms, and living rooms alike. We need pastors on their knees, not rehearsing TED Talks but interceding for fire from heaven. We need business leaders who dream with the Spirit, not only with spreadsheets. We need teenagers baptized in boldness before they ever step into baptismal waters.

Stockdale Paradox Christianity

•••••••••••••••••••••••••••••••••••••

We don't need another church growth manual. We don't need one more conference, podcast, or influencer. We need fire.

•••••••••••••••••••••••••••••••••••••

We need ordinary saints who know that their courage is supernatural, not self-made. We need the resurrection power of Jesus Christ unleashed again in homes, churches, schools, city councils, and Capitol Hill.

Righteousness can reign again, not if the church perfects its methods, but if the church bows in surrender to the crucified, risen, and ascended Christ. This is the mandate of the Kingdom Triangle, not as a theory but as a revolution: Spirit-filled, mind-renewed, soul-restored disciples who live ablaze with courage and conviction. And it is the only way we win.

As J. P. Moreland reminds us, "If we are going to do kingdom ministry, we must embrace a supernatural worldview and walk in the power of the Holy Spirit"[1] Without that worldview, without that power, we are simply building sandcastles against a rising tide. With it, we become a people who cannot be ignored, because heaven itself moves through us.

And E. M. Bounds, with prophetic clarity, presses the point further: "What the Church needs today is not more machinery or better, not new organizations or more novel methods, but men [and women] whom the Holy Ghost can use—men [and women] of prayer, men [and women] mighty in prayer."[2] His words echo across generations, reminding us that courage is not optional, it is commanded—and only Spirit-filled men and women of prayer will be strong enough to obey that command.

THE COURAGEOUS FINAL CHARGE

God never invited his people to courage—he commanded it. "Haven't I commanded you: be strong and courageous? Do not be afraid or discouraged, for the LORD your God is with you wherever you go" (Josh 1:9).

Courage has always been the line in the sand. Joshua called Israel to choose. Elijah thundered against wavering. Jesus warned of the wide and narrow roads. And now, here we stand in our own generation, staring down

---

1. Moreland, *Kingdom Triangle*, 176.
2. Bounds, *Power Through Prayer*, 5.

the same choice: Stockholm or Stockdale, compromise or courage, silence or Spirit fire.

We have traced the drift: how the church has slowly surrendered ground, traded altars for auditoriums, and let shepherds fall silent when the sheep needed a voice. We have seen the devastation of capitulation: pulpits neutered, classrooms hijacked, consciences muzzled. We've faced the brutal facts.

But we have also seen the way out. It is not found in Stockholm survival but in Stockdale surrender. It is the Kingdom Triangle fully alive: Spirit at the apex, mind renewed in truth, soul restored in wholeness. It is the presence of the Holy Spirit animating every vertex, every thought, every heartbeat, every action. Without him, the triangle is a diagram. With him, it is a revolution.

This is where Sisu comes in—not human grit alone, but holy resilience. The Spirit-filled people of God refusing to bow, digging deep, rising again and again with supernatural resolve. And this is progressive overload: every act of obedience strengthening the church's muscle, building capacity for greater faith, greater courage, greater glory.

· ·

This is not rhetorical—it is personal. History will remember whether we bowed or believed, whether we coasted or crashed. The Spirit is summoning a people who will not just admire Pentecost but embody it. The gates stand before you—now is the time to decide how you will live and how you will finish.

· ·

This is why we are here. We were not born for Stockholm captivity. We were born to be Stockdale Christians: resilient, Spirit-filled, advancing with unshakable hope. We were born for the rhino crash—to storm the gates of hell, not in arrogance or anger but in Spirit-anointed power that sets captives free.

The hunted have become the hunters. The fearful have become the faithful. The silenced have become the sent. Do not settle for survival when you were designed for victory. Do not drift when you were called to crash. The gates of hell do not yield to clever plans or polished personalities—they shatter before the church ablaze with the Spirit of the Living God.

"When they had prayed, the place where they were assembled was shaken, and they were all filled with the Holy Spirit and began to speak God's message with boldness" (Acts 4:31).

That same Spirit is still filling. Still shaking. Still sending. He is not looking for spectators—he is raising warriors.

So rise up.
Take your place.
Grip the cross.
Fix your eyes.
Engage the Kingdom Triangle.
Embrace holy Sisu.
Train in progressive overload.
Walk in the Spirit.
Crash the gates—rescue the captives.

And when history remembers this moment, may it be said of us that while others bowed, we stood. While others coasted, we crashed. While others ghosted, we burned with fire. The Spirit is calling. The gates are waiting. The hour is late.

Are you in?

EPILOGUE: A PRAYER OF COMMISSION

Father,

I lift up the one who has walked this journey, who has lingered over these pages and wrestled with the weight of your call. They are not here by accident. They are here because you summoned them. You have called them to stand when others bow, to burn when others grow cold, to live not in fear but in fire.

Holy Spirit,

Fall fresh upon them. Break every chain of hesitation, silence, or self-doubt. Let them know that you have not overlooked them. Fill their mind with truth that cannot be shaken, their soul with peace that cannot be stolen, and their heart with love that cannot run dry. Ignite in them holy Sisu: resilience that keeps rising, faith that keeps fighting, courage that keeps advancing.

Stockholm or Stockdale... the Choice is Yours!

Lord Jesus,

Be their vision, their strength, their joy. Let them walk as you walked—not avoiding the darkness but stepping into it with light. Let their home, their workplace, their classroom, their community become holy ground because they carry your Spirit wherever they go. May their prayers shake the heavens. May their words heal the broken. May their life crash the gates of hell and rescue captives who will one day join the chorus of heaven.

And now, beloved one:
Go in the power of the Spirit.
Go in the authority of the risen Christ.
Go in the love of the Father who delights in you.
You are not alone.
You are not powerless.
You are not insignificant.
You are filled.
You are chosen.
You are sent.
Rise, and stand while others bow.
Crash the gates, and set the captives free.
The Spirit is with you—always.

> *For God has not given us a spirit of fearfulness, but one of power, love, and sound judgment.*
> —2 Tim 1:7

> *No, in all these things we are more than victorious through Him who loved us.*
> —Rom 8:37

> *I will build My church, and the forces of Hades will not overpower it.*
> —Matt 16:18

To Christ be the glory, in his church and through his Spirit, now and forever. Amen.

Bibliography

Anderson, Ray S. *On Being Human: Essays in Theological Anthropology*. Eugene, OR: Wipf & Stock, 2010.
Augustine. *City of God*. Translated by Henry Bettenson. London: Penguin Classics, 2003.
Barna, George. *Think Like Jesus: Make the Right Decision Every Time*. Nashville: Nelson, 2003.
Barna Group. "Most American Christians Do Not Believe that Satan or the Holy Spirit Exist." Apr. 13, 2009. https://www.barna.com/research/most-american-christians-do-not-believe-that-satan-or-the-holy-spirit-exist.
———. "Pastors Face Communication Challenges in a Divided Culture." Jan. 29, 2019. https://www.barna.com/research/pastors-speaking-out/.
———."Signs of Decline and Hope Among Key Metrics of Faith." Mar. 4, 2020. https://www.barna.com/research/changing-state-of-the-church/.
Basham, Megan. *Shepherds for Sale: How Evangelical Leaders Traded the Truth for a Leftist Agenda*. New York: Broadside, 2024.
Bounds, E. M. *Power Through Prayer*. New Kensington, PA: Whitaker, 1982.
Brainerd, David. *The Life and Diary of David Brainerd*. Edited by Jonathan Edwards. New Haven: Yale University Press, 1949.
Bridges Johns, Cheryl. *Re-Enchanting the Text: Discovering the Bible as Sacred, Dangerous, and Mysterious*. Grand Rapids: Baker Academic, 2023.
Brother Andrew. *God's Smuggler*. With John Sherrill and Elizabeth Sherrill. Grand Rapids: Chosen, 2001.
Buckley, William F., Jr. *God and Man at Yale: The Superstitions of Academic Freedom*. Washington, DC: Regnery, 1951.
Burris, Glenn, Jr. "Important Reimagine Discussions at Connection 2014." Foursquare.org, Apr. 10, 2014. https://resources.foursquare.org/important_reimagine_discussions_at_connection_2014/.
Burton Edwards, Taylor W. "Part 5: Human Sexuality." The United Methodist Church (website), May 2024. https://www.umc.org/en/content/ask-the-umc-whats-new-in-the-book-of-discipline-part-5-human-sexuality.
Carlin, George. *George Carlin: You Are All Diseased*. Directed by Rocco Urbisci. Recorded Feb. 6, 1999. HBO Original Programming, 1999.
Carter, Joe. "9 Things You Should Know About the Bethel Church Movement." The Gospel Coalition, Sept. 29, 2018. https://www.thegospelcoalition.org/article/9-things-you-should-know-about-the-bethel-church-movement/.

Bibliography

Chan, Francis, and Danae Yankoski. *Forgotten God: Reversing Our Tragic Neglect of the Holy Spirit.* Colorado Springs, CO: Cook, 2009.

Clements, Jonathan. *Mannerheim: President, Soldier, Spy.* London: Haus, 2009.

Collins, Jim. *Good to Great: Why Some Companies Make the Leap . . . and Others Don't.* New York: HarperBusiness, 2001.

Cushman, Philip. *Constructing the Self, Constructing America.* New York: Perseus, 1995.

Deere, Jack. *Surprised by the Power of the Spirit.* Grand Rapids: Zondervan, 1993.

D'Souza, Dinesh. "Islam and Democracy." Season 5, episode 1096 in *The Dinesh D'Souza Podcast,* June 3, 2025. Featuring William Wolfe. 53:54. https://omny.fm/shows/dinesh-d-souza-podcast/islam-and-democracy.

Elmore, Tim. *Generation iY: Secrets to Connecting with Today's Teens and Young Adults in the Digital Age.* Atlanta, GA: Poet Gardner, 2010.

Fee, Gordon D. *God's Empowering Presence: The Holy Spirit in the Letters of Paul.* Peabody, MA: Hendrickson, 1994.

———. *Paul, the Spirit, and the People of God.* Grand Rapids: Baker Academic, 1996.

Finney, Charles G. *Lectures on Revivals of Religion.* Oberlin, OH: Goodrich, 1868.

———. *Memoirs of Rev. Charles G. Finney.* Edited by George Frederick Wright. New York: Barnes, 1876.

Frodsham, Stanley Howard. *Smith Wigglesworth: Apostle of Faith.* Springfield, MO: Gospel Publishing, 1948.

Goetz, Stewart, and Charles Taliaferro. *A Brief History of the Soul.* Malden, MA: Wiley-Blackwell, 2011.

Guinness, Os. *Fit Bodies, Fat Minds: Why Evangelicals Don't Think and What to Do About It.* Grand Rapids: Baker, 1994.

———. *A Free People's Suicide: Sustainable Freedom and the American Future.* Downers Grove, IL: IVP, 2012.

Harris, Sam. *Letter to a Christian Nation.* New York: Knopf, 2006.

Hawkins, Greg L., et al. *Reveal: Where Are You?* With a foreword by Bill Hybels. South Barrington, IL: Willow Creek, 2007.

Horton, Michael. "Joel Osteen and the Glory Story." Westminster Seminary California, Oct. 1, 2007. https://www.wscal.edu/resources/article/joel-osteen-and-the-glory-story/.

Irenaeus. *Against Heresies.* In vol. 1 of *The Ante-Nicene Fathers.* Translated by Alexander Roberts and William Rambaut. Edited by Alexander Roberts and James Donaldson. Buffalo, NY: Christian Literature, 1885.

Jackson, Bill. *The Quest for the Radical Middle: A History of the Vineyard.* Cape Town: Vineyard International, 1999.

Johnson, Bill. *When Heaven Invades Earth: A Practical Guide to a Life of Miracles.* Shippensburg, PA: Destiny Image, 2003.

Johnson, Jessica. *The Rise and Fall of Mars Hill.* Grand Rapids: Eerdmans, 2015.

Johnson, Steve W. *Renovation Project: Developing a Christian Worldview from a Construction Site.* New York: Book Marketeers, 2023.

Justin Martyr. *Dialogue with Trypho.* Translated by Thomas B. Falls. The Fathers of the Church. Washington, DC: Catholic University of America Press, 1948.

Kasdan, Lawrence, dir. *Grand Canyon.* Screenplay by Lawrence Kasdan and Meg Kasdam. Featuring Danny Glover, Steve Martin, and Kevin Kline. Los Angeles, CA: Twentieth Century Fox, 1991.

Bibliography

Keener, Craig S. *Acts: An Exegetical Commentary.* 4 vols. Grand Rapids: Baker Academic, 2012–2015.

———. *Gift and Giver: The Holy Spirit for Today.* Grand Rapids: Baker Academic, 2001.

———. *Miracles: The Credibility of the New Testament Accounts.* 2 vols. Grand Rapids: Baker Academic, 2011.

Kennedy, Anne. "Christian Idolatry? Evaluating Bethel Church and Bill Johnson." Christian Research Institute, July 30, 2025. https://www.equip.org/articles/christian-idolatry-evaluating-bethel-church-and-bill-johnson/.

King, Larry. "Interview with Joel Osteen." *Larry King Live*, CNN, June 20, 2005. Interview transcript. https://transcripts.cnn.com/show/lkl/date/2005-06-20/segment/01.

Kinnamon, David. "Six Reasons Why Young People Leave the Church." Compiled by Eric Reed. *Leadership Journal* (2012). https://www.christianitytoday.com/2012/01/youngleavechurch/.

Kraft, Charles H. *Christianity in Culture: A Study in Dynamic Biblical Theologizing in Cross-Cultural Perspective.* Maryknoll, NY: Orbis, 1979.

———. *Christianity with Power: Your Worldview and Your Experience of the Supernatural.* Ann Arbor, MI: Vine, 1989.

Lahti, Emilia. "Sisu: Transforming Barriers into Frontiers at the Limits of Human Experience." PhD diss., Aalto University School of Science, 2019.

Lentz, Carl. "Carl and Laura Lentz Open Up (About Everything . . .)." Episode 1 of *Lights On with Carl Lentz* podcast. Released June 4, 2024. Apple Podcasts, 1:09:00. https://podcasts.apple.com/us/podcast/carl-and-laura-lentz-open-up-about-everything/id1747789103?i=1000657781733.

Macchia, Frank D. *Baptized in the Spirit: A Global Pentecostal Theology.* Grand Rapids: Zondervan, 2006.

MacNutt, Francis. *The Healing Reawakening: Reclaiming Our Lost Inheritance.* Grand Rapids: Chosen, 2005.

———. *The Nearly Perfect Crime: How the Church Almost Killed the Ministry of Healing.* Grand Rapids: Chosen, 2005.

Malik, Charles H. "The Two Tasks." In *The Two Tasks of the Christian Scholar: Redeeming the Soul, Redeeming the Mind*, edited by William Lane Craig and Paul M. Gould, 285–96. Wheaton, IL: Crossway, 2007.

McConnell, Scott. "Pastors, Churches Face Major Shifts with Covid-19." Lifeway Research, Apr. 7, 2020. https://research.lifeway.com/2020/04/07/pastors-churches-face-major-shifts-with-covid-19/.

Metaxas, Eric. *Amazing Grace: William Wilberforce and the Heroic Campaign to End Slavery.* New York: HarperOne, 2007.

———. *Bonhoeffer: Pastor, Martyr, Prophet, Spy.* Nashville: Nelson, 2010.

Meyer, Joyce. *Battlefield of the Mind.* Tulsa, OK: Harrison, 1995.

———. *Beauty for Ashes: Receiving Emotional Healing.* New York: Warner Faith, 2003.

Miller, Donald E., and Tetsunao Yamamori, eds. *Global Pentecostal and Charismatic Healing.* Oxford: Oxford University Press, 2011.

Moltmann, Jürgen. *The Church in the Power of the Spirit: A Contribution to Messianic Ecclesiology.* Translated by Margaret Kohl. New York: Harper & Row, 1977.

Moreland, J. P. *Kingdom Triangle: Recover the Christian Mind, Renovate the Soul, Restore the Spirit's Power.* Grand Rapids: Zondervan, 2007.

Moreland, J. P., and Klaus Issler. *The Lost Virtue of Happiness: Discovering the Disciplines of the Good Life.* Colorado Springs, CO: NavPress, 2006.

Bibliography

Nathan, Rich, and Ken Wilson. *Empowered Evangelicals*. Ann Arbor, MI: Vine, 1995.

Newton, Phil A. "Church Growth and Church Health: Lessons from the Past." *Founders Journal* 75 (2009) 15–20.

Noll, Mark A. *The Scandal of the Evangelical Mind*. Grand Rapids: Eerdmans, 1994.

Palau, Luis. *Palau: A Life on Fire*. Grand Rapids: Zondervan, 2019.

Park, Andy. *The Worship Journey*. Seattle, WA: CreateSpace, 2014.

Perry, Matthew. *Friends, Lovers, and the Big Terrible Thing*. New York: Flatiron, 2022.

Plantinga, Cornelius, Jr. *Not the Way It's Supposed to Be: A Breviary of Sin*. Grand Rapids: Eerdmans, 1995.

Ponsonby, Simon. *Loving Mercy: How to Serve a Tender-Hearted Saviour*. Oxford: Monarch, 2012.

Postman, Neil. *Amusing Ourselves to Death: Public Discourse in the Age of Show Business*. New York: Penguin, 1985.

Pullinger, Jackie, and Andrew Quicke. *Chasing the Dragon*. London: Hodder & Stoughton, 1980.

Rader, Dotson. "Brad Pitt: A Life So Large." *Parade*, Oct. 7, 2007, 6–9.

Ranaghan, Kevin J. *Brother André: The Miracle Man of Montreal*. Notre Dame: Ave Maria, 1988.

Raymond, Nate. "Churches Can Endorse Political Candidates to Congregations, IRS Says." Reuters, July 8, 2025. https://www.reuters.com/legal/government/churches-can-endorse-political-candidates-congregations-irs-says-2025-07-08/.

Rosenberg, Benjamin. "Mid Vermont Christian School Girls Basketball Forfeits Playoff Game Rather than Compete Against Team with Transgender Player." Vtdigger, Feb. 27, 2023. https://vtdigger.org/2023/02/27/mid-vermont-christian-school-girls-basketball-forfeits-playoff-game-rather-than-compete-against-team-with-transgender-player/.

Sagan, Carl. *Pale Blue Dot: A Vision of the Human Future in Space*. New York: Random House, 1994.

Schaeffer, Francis A. *The Church at the End of the 20th Century*. Downers Grove, IL: IVP, 1970.

———. *The Great Evangelical Disaster*. Wheaton, IL: Crossway, 1984.

Shellnut, Kate. "A Tale of Two Calvary Chapels: Behind the Movement's Split." *Christianity Today*, March 2017. https://www.christianitytoday.com/2017/02/tale-of-two-calvary-chapel-movement-split-chuck-smith/.

Smith, Christian, and Melinda Lundquist Denton. *Soul Searching: The Religious and Spiritual Lives of American Teenagers*. Oxford: Oxford University Press, 2005.

Smith, James K. A. *You Are What You Love: The Spiritual Power of Habit*. Grand Rapids: Brazos, 2016.

Stark, Rodney. *The Rise of Christianity*. San Francisco: HarperOne, 1997.

Staub, Dick. *The Culturally Savvy Christian: A Manifesto for Deepening Faith and Enriching Popular Culture*. San Francisco: Jossey-Bass, 2007.

Stockdale, James B. *Courage Under Fire: Testing Epictetus's Doctrines in a Laboratory of Human Behavior*. Stanford, CA: Hoover Institution, 1993.

Stone, Roxanne. "US Pastors Grappling with COVID-19 Restrictions and Politics." Barna Group, Aug. 12, 2020. https://www.barna.com/research/pastors-covid19-restrictions/.

Trotter, William R. *A Frozen Hell: The Russo-Finnish Winter War of 1939–1940*. Chapel Hill, NC: Algonquin, 1991.

Bibliography

The United Methodist Church. *The Book of Discipline of the United Methodist Church 2016*. Nashville: United Methodist Publishing, 2016.

———. *The Book of Discipline of the United Methodist Church 2020/2024*. Nashville: United Methodist Publishing, 2024.

———. "Understanding General Conference 2024: Frequently Asked Questions and Resources." Western North Carolina Conference (website), May 4, 2024. https://www.wnccumc.org/understanding-general-conference-2024-faqs.

The View. "Hillsong Church Pastor Carl Lentz Explains Why He Spoke Out Against Donald J. Trump's Response to Charlottesville." Interview with Carl Lentz. Facebook, Oct. 30, 2017. Video, 1:45. https://www.facebook.com/TheView/videos/10154966298321524/.

Vitz, Paul C. *Faith of the Fatherless: The Psychology of Atheism*. San Francisco: Ignatius, 2013.

Weinschenk, Susan. "The Dopamine Seekers: Shopping, Dopamine, and Anticipation." *Psychology Today*, Oct. 21, 2015. https://www.psychologytoday.com/us/blog/brain-wise/201510/the-dopamine-seekers.

West, John G. *Stockholm Syndrome Christianity: Why Christian Leaders Are Failing—and What We Can Do About It*. Seattle, WA: Discovery Institute, 2025.

Willard, Dallas. *The Great Omission: Reclaiming Jesus's Essential Teachings on Discipleship*. San Francisco: HarperCollins, 2006.

———. *Renovation of the Heart: Putting on the Character of Christ*. Colorado Springs, CO: NavPress, 2002.

Wimber, John, and Kevin Springer. *Power Evangelism*. San Francisco: Harper & Row, 1986.

Wood, George O. "Pentecost: This Is Our Time." Address delivered at the 52nd General Council of the Assemblies of God, Phoenix, AZ, Aug. 9, 2011.

Yong, Amos. *The Spirit Poured Out on All Flesh: Pentecostalism and the Possibility of Global Theology*. Grand Rapids: Baker Academic, 2005.

www.ingramcontent.com/pod-product-compliance
Lightning Source LLC
Chambersburg PA
CBHW071425160426
43195CB00013B/1813